FOUR SEASONS

COOKBOOK

by Bea Smith

Four Seasons Cookbook

by Bea Smith

Published by
Avery Color Studios
Marquette, Michigan 49855

Typeset, printed and bound in the
United States of America by
Lake Superior Press, Inc.
Marquette, Michigan

Copyright 1993 by
Avery Color Studios
ISBN #932212-79-4
Library of Congress #93-72740

Cover Illustrations by
Mary Frey

To My Readers:

What a catastrophy it would be if all of our natural foods ripened at the same time. My goodness, how could our forefathers have made their pickles, canned their fruit and tomatoes, tapped the maples for sugar, picked the cherries, made apple cider—all at the same time? Not to mention the harvesting of the garden vegetables and the digging of the potatoes.

Mother nature has been very considerate; she has given us the "Four Seasons" to use and enjoy her bounties.

I feel very lucky to have been brought up on a family farm in the thumb area of Michigan, where we lived close to the soil and the four seasons. From maple syrup time to the first rhubarb, wild strawberries, garden vegetables and a big old orchard of apple, pear and cherry trees, I love to share mother's old-time recipes through the seasons with our modern easy-to-do recipes.

There are so many things that I am thankful for. My school years in Flint and my married years—living a number of years in Missouri, Ohio and Indiana, especially learning about the food in those wonderful places while raising our daughters Gloria and Shirley, then retiring to the north country, Walter's home area.

I am even grateful for my widowhood years—with time to spend writing my books and newspaper columns. This is a good time to express my thanks to my many friends and family who have made this all possible.

With love,

Bea

Beatrice McNiel Smith

Spring

Table of Contents

Spring

Buttermilk Pancakes

4 T. buttermilk blend
1 C. all-purpose flour
1 T. sugar
1 t. baking powder
1 t. soda

1/4 t. salt
1 egg
1 C. water
2 T. melted shortening or salad oil

Stir dry ingredients together in a mixing bowl. Add beaten egg to water and shortening or oil; beat just until batter is smooth. Do not over-beat. Drop from a spoon onto a hot greased griddle; cook until top is full of bubbles and underside is brown. Turn and brown other side.
Makes 10 4" pancakes

I found that these pancakes brown very quickly. I had my stove set for medium high and my smoke alarm went off. So go easy on the heat, the sugar in the recipe could make them brown faster than usual for pancakes.

Another delicious "Oldie." My grandmother, Wealthy Cramer (1852-1926) had to take her own jug to the store for molasses to be filled from a slow dripping barrel. It was a popular staple in those days.

Molasses Sauce for Pancakes

1/4 C. butter
1/2 C. molasses
Cream butter and molasses; heat.
Serve over pancakes with ham, bacon or crisp salt pork.

It's Maple Syrup Time

Freezing nights and thawing days brings the sap rising in the sugar maples. Even though they were hauling the buckets of sap through the snow to the sugar shanty with the horses and sleigh, the old-timers knew that Spring was just around the corner. That's when pancake suppers became a tradition in our Northern sugar bush areas.

To honor our old-timers, here is a tried-and-true recipe for pancakes with a new convenience; a dry cultured buttermilk blend. It is good for any recipe calling for liquid buttermilk using 4 level tablespoons to one cup of water.

It's Maple Syrup Time

I believe that I must be following in my father's footsteps; he could never have pancakes too often. What's better for a late winter or early spring supper than pancakes, hot apple sauce and maple syrup unless it is an individual soup bowl of maple syrup with flaky biscuits for dunking, the old-fashioned way.

Nutritionists will agree that pancakes are good for us, especially when we make them with whole wheat flour. I make them like this.

Marguerite's Mile High Biscuits

3 C. flour
1/8 C. plus 1/2 t. baking powder
3/4 t. cream of tartar
3/4 t. salt

2-1/2 T. sugar
3/4 C. shortening
1 egg, beaten
1 C. milk

Mix all dry ingredients; cut in the shortening and add the beaten egg and milk. Roll out on a lightly floured board to one inch in thickness. Cut with a 2 inch biscuit cutter or glass. Place about 1 inch apart on an ungreased cookie sheet and bake in a 450 degree oven for 15 minutes.

Whole Wheat Pancakes

1 C. graham flour (whole wheat)
1/2 C. all-purpose flour
1 t. soda
2 C. buttermilk

1 T. sugar
1/2 t. salt
2 t. melted shortening

Mix both flours with the salt and sugar. In another small bowl, dissolve the soda in the buttermilk. Mix all ingredients, adding the melted shortening. This is a thin batter. Fry on a hot griddle.

These are my favorite griddle cakes, light and fluffy. Spread them thin on the griddle. Sometimes I substitute 1 tablespoon of molasses for the sugar, adding it to the batter with the melted shortening.

That's right—there are no eggs in these pancakes.

Self-Rising Biscuits

For 12 biscuits, use:
2 C. self-rising flour
1 C. milk
4 T. mayonnaise (the real kind)

Stir up and pour into greased muffin tins or drop by spoonfuls onto a pan. Bake at 400 degrees 15 minutes or until lightly browned.

From Wilma Zoulek, East Jordan

It's Maple Syrup Time

One more biscuit recipe; the easiest biscuits I ever made, they raise high and are so very good.

3

A Touch of Spring

We need salads to beautify our meals as the days begin to lengthen. We are waiting for the crocus to push up through the snow and the arrival of the song birds to reassure us that Spring is really on the way. A bright touch of color to any salad is important now; add some sliced hard boiled eggs, sliced stuffed olives, a dab of jelly, a cherry or some bright yellow cheese. Bake some corn meal muffins for a colorful, nourishing luncheon. It's that added touch that makes all the difference. Many times it is what accompanies the dish that brings out its beauty, like this next recipe from Don Taylor.

Don's Chicken or Pork Curry

2 large chicken breasts or 4 one-inch thick pork chops
Salt and pepper to taste
1 C. rice
2 C. boiling water
2 chicken bouillon cubes
1-1/2 t. to 1 T. curry powder (go by your family's taste here)
Shredded coconut for garnish

Brown chops or chicken breasts lightly in just a little vegetable oil. Put into a heavy pot with a tight-fitting cover; sprinkle with rice, salt, pepper and curry powder. Dissolve bouillon cubes in boiling water; add to pot. Cover and cook slowly 1-1/2 hours, adding more hot water if it gets too dry. Makes 4 servings. Just before serving Don Sprinkles the dish with coconut.

This is delicious as it is, though very exciting when you surround it with the following version of Tomato Chutney:

Tomato Chutney

1 T. salad oil
1 whole red chili pepper, crumbled
1/2 t. cumin seed
1/4 t. nutmeg
1/4 t. mustard seed
4 medium tomatoes, peeled, sliced 1/2 inch thick
1/2 lemon, quartered
1/3 C. raisins
1/2 C. sugar

Heat oil, add chili pepper, cumin, nutmeg and mustard seed. Add tomatoes and lemons when seeds start to jump. Simmer, stirring frequently 30 minutes or until thickened. Chill, pack in sterilized jars, seal. Serve at room temperature.

Recipes like the above give me a terrific feeling of respect for the people of the countries from which they come.

A Touch of Spring

Surround your curry with small bowls of pickle relish, coconut, honey mixed with lemon juice, raisins and chutney. You can buy chutney or make this recipe from Bengal. It is sweeter and milder than most.

A Touch of Spring

Here is a beautiful salad, a perfect picture of the greens and yellows of Spring.

Orange and Avocado Salad

1/2 c. fresh lemon juice
2 avocados
3 medium oranges
Lettuce leaves

Pour lemon juice into shallow bowl. Peel avocado, cut crosswise into 1/4 inch slices. Remove seed as sliced. Dip slices in lemon juice to keep from turning dark. Peel oranges; cut crosswise in 1/2 inch slices.

Line serving bowl with lettuce leaves. Place alternate layers of orange and avocado slices and lettuce, ending with avocado slices. Serve with this:

Orange Mayonnaise

3/4 C. mayonnaise
1/4 C. orange juice
1/2 t. paprika

Mix the mayonnaise, orange juice and paprika. Serve with the above salad.

Pork and Potato Casserole

4 thick pork chops
1 C. mushroom soup, undiluted
1/2 C. sour cream
1/4 C. water
2 T. parsley
2 C. sliced potatoes
Salt and pepper to taste

Layer one half of the potatoes in a 4 quart dish; add pork chops. You can brown them slightly first if you wish. Mix remaining ingredients; pour over the top. Bake, covered in 375 degree oven 1-1/4 hours or until tender. You might want to remove the cover 15 minutes before they are done for a nice brown crust.

A Delicious Green Salad

Green lettuce leaves
Chunks of white cooked chicken
Lots of red and green grapes
Slices of celery
Thin sliced water chestnuts
Celery Seed Dressing (recipe follows)
Thin sliced roasted almonds

Consider the tastes and the number of your guests when determining ingredient amounts.

Serve a large ripe strawberry and a couple of small muffins of different varieties on each plate for a complete luncheon dish.

The Wearing of the Green

It's St. Patrick's Day again and it seems a good idea to serve some kind of potato dish for our Irish friends. I am sure that they will love this old-fashioned recipe.

I have a delicious salad recipe which I think will complement any St. Patrick's Day meal. Leave out the cooked chicken if fixing it for a side salad. This would be a good idea if you are baking the above pork chops.

The Wearing of the Green

Now, this is my idea of a real Irish dessert. My daughter, Gloria, makes this when she wants her guests to know that she can cook also; her husband does all of their cooking.

Celery Seed Dressing

1 C. sugar
1 t. flour
1 t. paprika
1/4 t. dry mustard

1/2 C. white vinegar
3/4 C. vegetable oil
2 t. celery seed

Stir sugar, flour, paprika and mustard together in saucepan. Whisk in vinegar, mixing well. Cook over medium heat until mixture comes to a boil, boil one minute. Let stand at room temperature for 30 minutes. Whisk in oil and celery seed. Store in covered jar at room temperature. Good on any fruit or green salad.

Creme de Menthe Sundae Topping

1/2 C. crushed pineapple and juice
1 C. sugar
1/2 C. light corn syrup
1/2 C. water
Dash of salt
Creme de Menthe for flavor
Ice Cream

Boil all the ingredients except the Creme de Menthe together until pineapple is clear. This takes some time. Simmer it after it comes to a boil, stirring occasionally. Let cool. Add 1/2 C. Creme de Menthe. Serve over ice cream.

This sauce will keep a long time if no one knows about it!

Irish Stew

2 lbs. mutton chops
8 potatoes
4 turnips
4 small onions

Place the chops in a stew pan, cover with boiling water and simmer one hour. Add turnips, onions and potatoes cut in pieces. Pour in nearly a quart of cold water; cover stew pan tightly, let it stew gently 'til vegetables are ready to mash and the better part of the gravy is absorbed; season with 2 teaspoons salt and 1/2 teaspoon pepper. Then place in a dish; serve it up hot.

Irish Stew For Two

1-1/2 lbs. lamb
2 onions, sliced
2 diced carrots
3 potatoes, cubed
Salt and pepper to taste
3 C. boiling water
2 T. flour

Cut lamb in cubes; put in kettle. Cover with boiling water; cook slowly until meat begins to tender. Add onions, carrots and potatoes. Simmer until meat and vegetables are tender; season with salt and pepper. Mix flour with small amount of water to make a paste; stir into stew.

Serve with dumplings.

The Wearing of the Green

Some Irishmen and would-be Irishmen might even color their hair green and drink green beer on St. Patrick's Day. They will need a couple of recipes for:

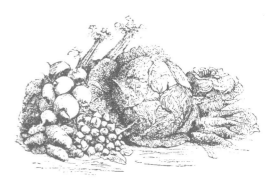

It seems that it does not make too much difference what vegetables you use. Years ago there were old jokes about what went into Irish stew. Remember the song, "Who put the overalls in Mrs. Murphy's chowder?"

Easter Season Celebrates New Life

April lies on the land, although sometimes patches of snow are seen on the hillsides leaving many shades of green; light green where the sun is shining, dark green in the shadows. I am thrilled with the tantalizing scent of new growth outside my patio door. How those first signs of Spring excite us.

A tradition has started and our family seems to think that we must have ham for Easter dinner. To accompany the ham we will have Barbie's potato casserole as well as candied yams and I would like oriental salad. We must have eggs in some form.

Barbie's Cheese Potatoes

1 pkg. (8 ozs.) sharp Cheddar cheese
1 bag frozen hash browns, thawed
1 container (16 ozs.) sour cream
1 can cream of chicken soup
1 small onion, chopped fine
3 T. butter
Salt and pepper to taste

Mix all ingredients except butter and salt in a 9 by 13 inch pan. Dab with butter and sprinkle with salt and pepper. Bake 45 minutes in 350 degree oven.

Oriental Salad

1 lb. fresh spinach, washed
1 can water chestnuts, drained and sliced
3/4 c. drained bean sprouts
1/2 lb. fried bacon, crumbled
3 hard boiled eggs

Dressing

1 small onion, chopped
1/2 C. oil
1/2 C. sugar
1/6 cup catsup
2 T. vinegar
1 T. Worcestershire sauce

Toss salad ingredients together. Mix dressing ingredients; add to salad. Toss and serve.

Magic Yams

1 can (16 ozs.) sliced cling peaches
1 T. cornstarch
1/2 C. packed brown sugar
1 can (8 ozs.) whole cranberry sauce
1/2 t. cinnamon
2 T. butter
2 cans (17 ozs.) each canned yams, drained

Drain peaches, reserving juice. Dissolve cornstarch in 1/4 C. of peach juice and set aside. Heat remaining juice, brown sugar, cranberry sauce, cinnamon and butter in 11-inch skillet. Add cornstarch mixture when butter is melted. Stir over medium heat until mixture thickens; add yams. Cover, cook 10 minutes. Stir in peaches; cook 5 minutes or until heated through.

Strawberry Mint Pie

1 pkg. vanilla pudding and pie filling
Few drops of peppermint extract
Few drops of green food coloring
1 baked pie shell
2 C. fresh strawberries
1/4 C. powdered sugar

Prepare vanilla pudding and pie filling according to package directions. Add peppermint extract and green food coloring. Do this carefully—not too much color. Cook five minutes; pour into baked pie shell. Chill. Dust whole or sliced strawberries with powdered sugar; arrange on top of pie.

Happy Easter!

Easter Season Celebrates New Life

If there could possibly be an improvement on candied yams, this next recipe would be it. It is something very special as an accompaniment for Easter ham.

Easter is a time for a special dessert and this one is beautiful, tasty and so easy to make.

Fishing Season

It seems that is is always fishing season somewhere in our beautiful country. My friend, Gorham Bird, works for a fisherman's supply company and a year ago he took a business tour to Alaska. How he loved it. He said that it was a hard job, but someone had to do it. How lucky can some people get? I am lucky too; Edna Brown gave me a new cookbook with some of her recipes in it called "Bellaire's Kitchen Secrets II." Here are some recipes for fish.

Try this next recipe for something different; it's so good.

Oven-Fried Fish

By Jean Thornell—Jean says "This is my favorite way of cooking fish. It cuts down on the fat content. I like to sprinkle a little lemon juice on the fish before I roll it in the crumbs."

4 fish fillets
1 egg
1/4 C. milk
1 to 3 C. cornflake crumbs, crushed

Cover pan with foil; spray lightly with cooking spray. Beat egg and milk. Wash fish; pat dry. Dip them in egg mixture; roll in crumbs. Place on foil. Bake in 400 degree oven until fish is flaky and brown.

What could be easier? I like a green vegetable and a lemony dessert with fish.

Salmon Pizza

1 can (7.75 ozs) pink salmon
Milk
2 C. biscuit mix
1 can (7.5 ozs.) tomato sauce
12 ozs. mozzarella cheese
1 C. minced onion

1/2 C. ripe olives, minced
1/4 C. chopped green peppers
1/4 t. oregano
Salt and pepper, to taste
1/4 C. grated Parmesan cheese

Drain salmon, reserving liquid. Add enough milk to reserved liquid to make 1/2 cup; blend with biscuit mix to make soft dough. Knead several times; roll into 12-inch circle. Fit into pizza pan. Spread dough with tomato sauce; layer with thin slices mozzarella cheese, flaked salmon, onion, olives and green pepper. Season with oregano, salt and pepper. Top with Parmesan cheese. Bake in 450 degree oven 15-20 minutes. Makes 3-4 servings.

Rainbow Trout Melt

From "Updated Family Recipes"
4 trout fillets
2 tomatoes
8 slices cheese

Garnishes:
Rye Toast Points
Red onion slices
Lettuce
Pickles

Broil trout 4 inches from heat source 3-5 minutes or until fish flakes with fork. Remove from broiler; top each fillet with 2-3 slices tomato and 2 slices cheese. Broil until cheese melts. Garnish with above suggestions. Makes 4 servings.

Fishing Season

Whether you are lucky enough to catch some rainbow trout, someone gives you a mess or even if you have to go to the market for some, you will love this:

Springtime Favorites

My friends, Bill and Lila Meyers of Clearwater, Florida, have given me some wonderful ideas for springtime cooking. Bill likes to reminisce about his early days in Northern California when he cooked for his father and two brothers. He talks of roast leg of lamb, hams, fresh pork with potatoes and gravy and pancakes made with applesauce for the liquid, flavored with vanilla, which he served with sausage or bacon and eggs. His wife, Lila, suggested this dip for any get-together.

Artichoke Dip

1 can (#25) artichoke hearts
1/2 C. grated Parmesan cheese
1 C. light mayonnaise

Combine all ingredients in blender until smooth. Place in baking dish; bake in 350 oven until bubbly. Serve on hot chips. Delicious!

If you are having a brunch instead of a dinner, Lila likes this omelette:

Oven Omelette

8 eggs
1/2 C. sour cream
3/4 t. salt
1 C. shredded Swiss cheese
2 lbs. green onions, chopped
6 slices Canadian bacon
2 T. melted butter

Beat eggs with sour cream and salt, add cheese and onions. Turn into 6 buttered individual baking dishes. Top with Canadian bacon slices; drizzle with melted butter. Bake in 350 degree oven 20 minutes or until set. This omelette can also be baked in a 9 x 13 inch baking pan.

Lila's Snowballs

1 C. melted Crisco
1/2 C. sifted powdered sugar
2-1/4 C. sifted flour
1/4 t. salt
3/4 C. finely chopped nuts—she likes pecans for this.

Cool melted shortening slightly; combine all ingredients in order given. Roll into balls about 3/4 inches in diameter. Place on cookie sheet; bake in 350 degree oven 10 to 15 minutes until lightly brown. Roll in powdered sugar when cool enough to handle.

Springtime Favorites

For either dinner or brunch finish the meal with strawberry shortcake or any fruit and this dessert.

Rhubarb Cake

The first "fruity" taste of spring must be rhubarb. How welcome this fruit or vegetable was to the old-timers just when most of the canned fruit from the cellar was all gone and before strawberries were ripe. They called it "Pie Plant." How we cherished Mother's first rhubarb pie of the season. She made it the same way that she made apple pie, with two crusts and lots of sugar.

I discovered a very special rhubarb cake at Milliken's tea room in downtown Traverse City. Shirley Caplinger, the tea room manager, very graciously had the recipe written out for me. This cake is delicious as is, though Shirley says that it is even better with a scoop of ice cream. Anyone who likes rhubarb will love this dessert.

Rhubarb Cake

3 lbs. rhubarb or enough to fill a 13 x 9 inch pan 2/3 full, cut in 1/2 inch pieces
1 C. firmly packed brown sugar
3/4 C. flour
1-1/4 lb. yellow cake mix
1 C. butter, melted
1 C. nuts

Combine first 3 ingredients; place in greased 13 x 9 inch pan. Combine cake mix and butter just until moistened; add nuts. Spread cake mix over rhubarb mixture in pan. Bake in 325 degree oven 45 minutes or until golden brown.

Asparagus Almondine

1 pkg. (12 ozs.) frozen chopped asparagus or 1 lb. fresh, cut in pieces
4 T. butter
4 T. almonds, slivered and blanched
2 T. pimiento, chopped
1/4 t. salt
Parsley

Steam asparagus until barely done; drain. Melt butter, stir in almonds. Cook until lightly browned. Add asparagus to buttered almonds; saute until thoroughly heated. Lay on serving dish, sprinkle with pimiento and parsley. Makes 4 to 5 servings.

Asparagus and chicken are good teammates; try this casserole.

Asparagus and Chicken Casserole

2 large chicken breasts
2 C. water
1 bay leaf
1 can cream of celery soup
1-1/2 lbs. fresh asparagus
Salt and pepper to taste
Parmesan cheese

Simmer chicken with bay leaf in water 1 hour, cool. Remove from bone; cut into bite-size portions. Cook fresh asparagus in boiling water until just slightly crisp; drain. Lay asparagus, chicken and soup in casserole dish; sprinkle with Parmesan cheese. Bake in 450 degree oven 20 minutes.

Asparagus

What is Spring without an asparagus bed? Early Michigan settlers brought their asparagus with them and planted it where it would not be dug up every year. A healthy bed of asparagus could last as long as 35 years. Our pioneers were always looking to the future when they planted their orchards, fields and gardens.

Although we pay a little more for asparagus than for some other vegetables, we should feel that we do get our money's worth when we realize that it takes 3 years for the plants to mature and it is picked by hand and marketed at once, as it is perishable. It is also rich in vitamins, minerals and has only 4 calories per spear cooked or raw. Treat your family with this asparagus almondine, with either frozen or fresh; it is easy, delicious and beautiful.

Asparagus

I like to cook asparagus just for myself in a glass pie pan in the microwave with the stalks on the outside and the tips in the center. Cook to tender crisp; serve with butter, salt and pepper—try a little squeeze of lemon.

If you want a fancy dish, prepare this:

Asparagus Supreme

1-1/2 lbs. asparagus
1 can cream of chicken soup
1/2 C. sour cream
2 T. melted butter
2 T. flour
1/2 C. grated carrot
1 T. grated onion
3/4 C. herb-seasoned stuffing mix
Salt and pepper to taste

Cut asparagus in 1 inch pieces; steam, microwave or cook in boiling water until tender. Blend soup and flour; add sour cream, carrot and onion. Stir in asparagus. Turn into a 2-quart baking dish. Combine stuffing mix and butter; spread around edge of dish. Bake in 350 degree oven for 30 minutes.

Wilted Lettuce and Onion Salad

8 slices bacon
1/2 C. vinegar
1/2 C. water
1 t. sugar
8 green onions, cut in small pieces
A good sized bowl of crisp leaf lettuce

Fry, cool and crumble bacon into pieces. Add vinegar, water and sugar to bacon drippings in skillet. Bring to boil; pour over lettuce and onions.

Top with crumbled bacon.

Stir-Fries

Stir-fry is in; it seems that its popularity increases daily. This is not a fad that will go away, because it is basic. They have been stir-frying in the Orient for hundreds of years. This method of cooking is healthful because we do not cook away all of those precious vitamins and minerals. We have learned to enjoy our veggies tender-crisp. Grandmother had her stir-fries, but she was of the opinion that vegetables needed to be cooked longer.

Mother made this next recipe when the first tender leaf lettuce was abundant in her garden and the green onions were young. It is almost a stir-fry.

Stir-Fries

Enjoy this next stir-fry with chop sticks if you are adept with them.

Vegetable and Beef Stir-Fry

1 can (20 oz.) pineapple chunks in natural juice
1/4 C. soy sauce
2 T. red wine vinegar
1-1/2 T. cornstarch
4 T. vegetable oil
1 lb. sirloin tip steak
2 C. broccoli flowerets
1 C. carrots, thinly sliced
1 medium onion, cut in wedges
1/2 medium red pepper cut in strips
Instant or long-grain rice

Drain pineapple; reserve juice. Combine juice, soy sauce, vinegar and cornstarch; set aside. Thinly slice beef across grain, cut into 1-1/2 inch strips. Heat 2 tablespoons oil in uncovered wok over high heat 2 minutes; add meat. Stir-fry 3 to 5 minutes or until browned. Remove beef and juices. Heat remaining oil; add vegetables. Stir-fry 2 to 3 minutes. Add juice mixture; stir until thickened. Stir in pineapple chunks and meat. Cover, cook 2 minutes. Serve with hot rice.

4 to 6 servings

Glazed Carrots and Onions

1 lb. carrots, peeled and cut into slices
3 medium to large onions, quartered
1/4 C. low-cholesterol margarine
2 T. brown sugar
1 t. ground ginger
1/2 t. salt

Melt margarine in large skillet or wok; add carrots and onions. Stir-fry on medium high 5 minutes, stirring constantly. Turn heat down to medium if it starts to brown. Add brown sugar, ginger and salt; continue stir-frying until carrots are glazed, 2 minutes.

4 servings

Stir-Fries

You can use large carrots cut into thick slices for this recipe. In that case, partially cook them a few minutes before stir-frying. I used small carrots and sliced them thin, so I did not pre-cook them. The carrots cooked beautifully and were delicious.

Power in the Potato

It's time now to find those luscious new red and white potatoes on the market. I hunger for them these spring days. They bring back a bit of nostalgia. In my memory I see Mother draining the potato water into the pan in which she had fried pork, beef or chicken, to make gravy. She had already browned a little flour in the pan with the drippings. She was not familiar with the vitamins and minerals then, but she knew that there was a lot of power in the potato. It is difficult to believe that our forefathers did without our number one vegetable before the 16th century.

Could there be a new recipe for potatoes? This one is new to me. If you have found some delicious morels use them here.

Fresh Potato Mushroom Bake

4 medium potatoes
2 t. salt, divided
2 T. butter or margarine
1/2 C. chopped fresh onion
1/4 t. paprika
1/2 lb. fresh mushrooms
2 C. (1/2 lb.) shredded Swiss cheese
4 eggs
2 C. milk
1/8 t. black pepper

Cover potatoes with water in large saucepan; add 1 teaspoon salt. Cover; bring to boil. Simmer 20 minutes or until potatoes are tender. Drain, peel and slice potatoes. Melt butter in large skillet; add onion and paprika. Cook until onion is tender. Add mushrooms and cook 5 minutes. Place layer of potatoes in greased 2-quart baking dish; top with half of the mushroom mixture; sprinkle with half the cheese. Repeat with the remaining potatoes, mushrooms and cheese. Beat eggs, milk and remaining salt and pepper together in large bowl, pour over vegetables in baking dish. Bake in 325 degree oven 50 to 60 minutes or until custard is set. Serves 4.

Garden Topped Potatoes

4 large potatoes
1/4 C. butter or margarine
2 medium onions, chopped
1 green pepper, cut in strips
1 clove garlic, minced
2 tomatoes, peeled, cut in wedges
1 small zucchini, sliced
1/3 C. grated Parmesan cheese
1/4 t. salt
Pinch of black pepper
8 ozs. plain yogurt

Wash and prick potatoes, bake in 450 degree oven 40 to 50 minutes. Turn oven off; prepare vegetable topping.

Melt butter in large skillet; saute onion, green pepper and garlic until tender-crisp, 3 minutes. Stir in tomatoes and zucchini; cook, stirring often, 2 minutes. Stir in Parmesan cheese, salt, pepper and yogurt; continue cooking, stirring constantly, 1 minute.

Split top of baked potatoes, fluff with fork. Spoon on vegetable mixture. Makes 4 servings.

Power in the Potato

This next recipe uses baking potatoes for a colorful and delicious meal.

A Few Notes on the Potato— The King of Vegetables

Put a few slices of those new potatoes in the pan when stir-frying garden vegetables.

They are good boiled with a sprig of mint; it gives them a delicious flavor without over-powering the fresh potato taste.

Just remember that plain boiled potatoes are good with a variety of seasonings. Mix butter with freshly chopped chives, scallions or other herbs to add flavor. I like a little dill or parsley.

Farmer's Wife in Poultry Business

What a difference a few years make. Remember when chicken was more expensive than meat?

Sunday Dinner

Mother usually had to choose between the old hen that had quit laying or a young rooster; quite often the hen was tough, so she stewed it and then fried it in butter to brown. Then what delicious gravy she made from that fry pan. She always made biscuits or had home-made rolls. She roasted stuffed whole chicken for Thanksgiving and Christmas. Here is the old fashioned way to make:

Stewed Chicken

Put the chicken, cut in pieces or whole in boiling water; let the water boil for 15 minutes. Then add (for an average sized bird) 1 tablespoon salt. Let the chicken continue to cook at a simmering temperature for 1-1/2 hours, or until tender. Serve with gravy using 1/4 cup flour to two cups of broth. Mother made this gravy after browning the pieces in the frying pan, sometimes she added some cream to the gravy—Yummy!

My niece, Nellie, is one of many farm women who still raise their own poultry. She and her husband, Armond, dress enough chickens at a time to last them for a year in their freezer. This is the way Nellie prepared chicken when I visited them.

Nellie's Chicken

2 fryers or broilers, whole or cut into large pieces
1 T. non-cholesterol shortening or oil
1/2 bottle of Ranch-type salad dressing
Salt to taste (optional)

Nellie and Armond are cholesterol and fat-free conscious people, so they remove the skins when butchering their chickens.

Brown meat in Dutch oven or large heavy skillet with tight fitting cover, brush with salad dressing. Cover; cook slowly at lower heat one hour or until tender, turning meat occasionally. This chicken was tender and so very delicious.

Festive Chicken

2 lbs. chicken parts
2 T. shortening
1 can (14-1/2 ozs.) chicken broth
1 medium clove garlic, minced
2 t. soy sauce
1/2 t. ginger
4 medium size carrots, very thinly sliced diagonally
1 pkg. (6 ozs.) frozen Chinese pea pods
1/4 C. water
1 T. cornstarch
Cooked rice

Brown chicken in shortening in skillet; pour off fat. Add broth, garlic, soy sauce and ginger. Cover; cook over low heat 35 minutes. Add carrots; cook 10 minutes or until done, stirring occasionally. Add pea pods. Combine water and cornstarch; slowly stir into sauce. Cook stirring, until thickened.

Serve with rice and additional soy sauce. Makes 6 servings.

Farmer's Wife in Poultry Business

Here is a tasty dish using canned chicken broth. I think that my creative Mother would have liked this recipe.

Farmer's Wife in Poultry Business

Mother's Poultry Business

The greatest food revolution in history has been right under our nose over the last 50 years, and nowhere has it been more pronounced than in the poultry business.

Every spring one could hear the peeping of the little chicks in post offices throughout Michigan and all of the Midwest. People sent to Sears Roebuck and other places for baby chicks to be fed and cared for until they were ready to be sold as broilers or raised for laying hens. The farmer's wife was in the poultry business.

Turkey With Peppers

1 T. light brown sugar, packed
1 T. soy sauce
2 t. cornstarch
1 C. cooked turkey, chicken or pork, cubed
2 T. oil
1 T. finely chopped garlic
1 med. red pepper, cut in 1-inch chunks
1 med. green pepper, cut in 1-inch chunks
4 green onions, cut in one inch pieces

Combine brown sugar, soy sauce and cornstarch; add turkey and turn over to coat. Heat oil in large skillet; cook garlic and turkey mixture over high heat 3 minutes, stirring constantly. Stir in peppers and onions; cook over medium high heat, stirring constantly, 5 minutes or until vegetables are tender-crisp.

Serve on rice or noodles. Makes 4 servings.

Here is another delicious recipe from my friend, Wealtha Hedgecock. It's a quickie using left-over turkey.

Caramel Cheesecake Flan

3/4 C. sugar
2 pkg. (8 ozs. each) cream cheese, softened
1 can (13 ozs.) sweetened condensed milk (not evaporated)
4 eggs
1-1/2 t. vanilla
1/2 t. salt
1 C. water

Preheat oven to 350 degrees. Cook sugar in heavy skillet over medium heat, until melted and caramel-colored, stirring constantly. Pour into ungreased 9 inch round layer cake pan, tilting to coat bottom completely.

Beat cheese in large mixer bowl until fluffy; gradually beat in sweetened milk until smooth. Add eggs, vanilla and salt; mix well. Add water gradually on low speed until smooth; pour into carmelized pan.

Set in larger pan (a broiler pan); fill pan with one inch of hot water. Bake 55 to 60 minutes or until top springs back when lightly touched. Cool. Invert onto serving plate with rim. Garnish as desired, a few sliced strawberries in the center are beautiful.

Mother's Day

Janet Waldner, our town librarian, gave me the following recipe some time ago and I have saved it for Mother's Day. It is a favorite dessert of several members of her family. I hope someone makes it for Janet, who is really an international gourmet. She travels extensively to visit her children in far-away places and loves Mexican foods. Here is a recipe for a flan, which is a classic Mexican dessert.

Mother's Day

Mother would be impressed if you made this special:

Microwave Chicken Kiev

1-1/2 lbs. skinless, boneless chicken breasts (4 to 6 pieces)
4-6 T. frozen and sliced butter
2/3 C. fine bread crumbs
1/3 C. grated Parmesan cheese
1 T. fresh chopped parsley
1 t. paprika
1/4 t. garlic salt
1 egg
3 T. flour
1/4 t. pepper

Pound chicken breasts until 3/4 thick. Place 1 slice frozen butter on each pounded chicken breast; roll up lengthwise tucking ends under. Set aside.

Mix bread crumbs, cheese, parsley, paprika and garlic salt together in small bowl. Beat egg in separate small bowl. Combine flour and pepper on plate; stir with fork to mix. Dredge chicken breast rolls in flour and pepper mixture; dip into beaten egg, then roll in bread crumb mixture. Arrange breast rolls in 10-inch flat microwave-safe casserole dish; cover loosely with plastic wrap.

Microwave on medium-high 12 to 17 minutes or until chicken is no longer pink, rotating dish a couple of times. Let stand, covered, 10 minutes before serving.

Great Granola

1-1/2 C. rolled oats
1/4 C. sunflower seeds
1/8 C. wheat germ
1/8 t. cinnamon
1/8 C. honey
3 T. safflower oil
1/2 C. chopped dried apples or other dried fruit
1/2 C. raisins

Preheat oven to 350 degrees. Combine oats, sunflower seeds, wheat germ and cinnamon in large bowl. Stir honey and oil together, pour over oat mixture, tossing to coat dry ingredients. Spread mixture in shallow 9 x 13 inch pan; bake on middle rack of oven 15 minutes, stirring frequently. Allow to cool. Stir dried fruit into cooled granola. Store in covered container in refrigerator.

Makes 11 quarter cup servings. A decorated coffee can is great for this. Mom will love it.

Mother's Day

If you want to give Mother a special little gift of love, you can make something that even the young children can help prepare. She will think of you every morning when she eats this granola.

Father's Day

On Father's Day many seniors are carried back in time, thinking about their fathers. We like to reminisce and when I say to my daughters, "Just like your father," or to my grandson, "Just like your grandfather," it is an expression of love.

We understand our fathers now, since we have been through their problems in our own experiences. Through the years I have heard my husband say that he wished that he had been better acquainted with his father, who left this earth when Walter was in his early 20s. I am sure that many of us feel the same way. This is one of his favorite recipes which he copied and dated, Nov. 15, 1969.

Walter's Pork Chops

Brown 4 pork chops; season with salt and pepper. Put in a shallow baking pan; add 1 can of tomato soup. Slice stuffed olives on top. Cover with foil; bake in 350 degree oven 45 to 60 minutes or until very tender. So simple and so good!

This next recipe is my grandson's favorite. Joe says that I do not need to make it every time he comes, but he expects it occasionally, as it has all of his favorite foods in one dish.

Stuffed Potatoes a la Reuben

6 large baking potatoes
oil
1/4 C. milk
1 can (8 oz.) sauerkraut
1-1/2 C. diced, cooked corned beef
salt and pepper
Mustard Cheese Sauce (recipe follows)

Scrub potatoes, rub lightly with oil. Pierce several times with fork; bake in 400 degree oven 50 to 60 minutes or until tender. Cut lengthwise slice from top of each potato; scoop out pulp, mash with butter and milk, add sauerkraut, corned beef, salt and pepper to taste; spoon mixture into shells. Return to oven; bake 15 to 20 minutes. Serve with the following sauce.

Mustard Cheese Sauce

3 T. butter or margarine
3 T. flour
1 T. prepared mustard
1/2 t. salt
Dash of pepper and Worcestershire sauce
1/2 C. milk
1 C. shredded Swiss cheese

Melt butter or margarine in saucepan; blend in flour, prepared mustard, salt, pepper, Worcestershire sauce and milk. Cook and stir until thickened. Stir in cheese, heat until melted. Makes 2 cups.

Father's Day

Father's Day

Dessert? Of course, for Father's Day. Ruth Ann Biggs made this luscious dessert, worthy of any father, for a lovely dinner at their home in Marshall last summer. It was served at the Hyatt Regency Hilton Head kitchen tour of homes, March 30, 1991.

Hemingway's Fresh Fruit Cobbler

1 C. flour
1 C. sugar
1 egg
1 t. vanilla
2 t. lemon juice
1 t. baking soda
2/3 C. milk
1-1/2 C. fresh chopped fruit to include favorite fruits on hand like pears, pineapple, strawberries, blueberries, raspberries and bananas.
1 T. butter
1/4 C. cinnamon sugar, divided

Mix flour, 1 C. sugar and baking soda together in medium bowl. Mix egg, milk, vanilla and lemon juice in another bowl; pour into flour mixture. Mix until blended. Chop fruit into raspberry size pieces. Grease small glass casserole or 9 inch smooth pie pan with 1 tablespoon butter; add cinnamon sugar to pan—swirl out excess butter. Add chopped fruit except bananas; cover fruit with batter. Put sliced bananas on top of batter; sprinkle with cinnamon sugar.

Bake in 325 degree oven 20 to 25 minutes or until done. Use toothpick to test for doneness in center. Let rest 5 minutes before serving. Makes 4 generous servings.

The fruit can be chopped and mixed ahead of time, though do not mix strawberries, raspberries, or blueberries until the last minute.

Summer

Summer is upon us; how we yearned for Spring. . .then Summer suddenly arrived before we knew it! When strawberries are ripe, we 'Think Summer.'

Table of Contents

Summer

9-Minute Strawberry Jam

2 qts. strawberries
6 C. white sugar

Clean the strawberries; pour boiling hot water over them. Set one minute, drain off water. Put on stove; bring to a boil. Boil 3 minutes, then add 3 cups of sugar; bring to a boil, boiling for 3 minutes. Add the remaining 3 cups of sugar; bring to a boil, cooking 3 minutes.

Set aside; let cool—sometimes overnight. This thickens as it cools. Pour into glasses the next day and seal with wax.

Strawberries even make delicious salads. Like this:

Strawberry Tossed Salad

4 C. torn salad greens
1 C. watercress, if available
1 C. sliced fresh strawberries
1/2 small red onion, sliced thin
1/4 C. purchased or homemade Poppy Seed Dressing (recipe follows) or oil and vinegar dressing

Strawberries

Strawberries need no special adornment, they are nature's perfect fruit just the way they are. We like them with their caps on, surrounding a little pile of powdered sugar on a small plate. Dunk them in the sugar and enjoy. If you have not dunked them in sour cream, then brown sugar, you have really missed something!

This is the way my friend, Wealtha Hedgecock, makes her old-fashioned strawberry jam. She says that a friend gave her this recipe more than 35 years ago. They went berry picking together and she has been making this jam for years, successfully with both tame and wild strawberries.

Strawberries

Try this beautiful salad with my Poppy Seed Dressing:

Poppy Seed Dressing

1 bottle (8 oz.) red wine vinegar
1/2 C. sugar
1/2 t. dry mustard
1-1/2 t. grated grapefruit peel
1/2 C. grapefruit juice
2 T. poppy seeds

Combine all ingredients in container of electric blender; cover and blend well. Refrigerate several hours before serving. Makes 1-1/2 cups of very special salad dressing! Good on any fruit salad.

Sunburst Spinach Salad

2 ruby red grapefruit
1/2 lb. fresh spinach, torn into bite size pieces
1 pt. fresh strawberries

Combine grapefruit sections, spinach and strawberries in bowl; toss gently. Serve immediately with Poppy Seed Dressing. Makes 6 servings.

Strawberry Rhubarb Pie

1-1/2 pts. strawberries, washed, hulled and halved
2 C. sliced fresh rhubarb
1-1/2 C. sugar
6 T. quick-cooking tapioca
Unbaked pastry for double pie crust (buy or make)
Milk as needed
Sugar as needed

Mix strawberries and rhubarb with sugar and tapioca; let stand while preparing the crust. I have to admit that I buy the deep, unbaked pie crust for this. Following the directions on the package for a double crust pie.

Pour fruit into pie shell, put on top crust and seal edges. Brush with milk and sprinkle with sugar. Bake in 400 degree oven 60 to 70 minutes or until bubbly in the center. After 30 minutes of baking, check pie occasionally and cover edges with foil, if necessary, to prevent browning. Cool thoroughly before cutting. Top each piece with vanilla ice cream if you want to gild a lily!

Here is a beautiful quickie:

Strawberry Angel

Split a purchased angel-food cake in half crosswise. Spread top of one section with fresh or frozen sliced strawberries; cover with sweetened whipped cream or whipped topping and fill center with sweetened strawberries.
8 servings.

Strawberries

I like this suggestion from the American Dairy Association:

Place hulled strawberries in the work bowl of a food processor or blender; cover. Process until smooth. Add confectioners' sugar for a sweeter taste and a dash of lemon juice to heighten the flavor. Drizzle over ice cream or pound cake.

The Fourth of July

It would not be the Fourth of July without fried or barbecued chicken, new potatoes and peas and, of course, strawberry shortcake. Homemade ice cream also comes to mind. Everyone in our town goes to the big parade downtown which ends at the city park where the Lion's Club has been roasting chickens for hours. There is a long line for the chicken, but it is worth it. We can eat it there or take it home, where we will serve it with our favorite summer dishes.

New Potatoes and Peas

I like to cook the peas and potatoes separately because somtimes it takes a little longer to cook those new potatoes and we do not want the peas over-cooked. In the meantime, make a rich white sauce:

White Sauce

2 T. butter or margarine
2 T. flour
2 C. milk
Salt and pepper to taste

Melt the butter in a heavy saucepan or skillet; add the flour and stir until smooth. Gradually add the milk, stirring constantly. Cook until smooth and thick. Season with salt and pepper.

Drain the peas and potatoes and add to the sauce and heat through, with a final seasoning of salt and pepper to your taste.

Strawberry Shortcake

1 qt. strawberries, hulled and sliced
1/2 C. sugar

Biscuits

2 C. flour
4 t. baking soda
1/4 C. sugar
1/2 t. salt
5 heaping T. shortening
1 C. buttermilk

Combine strawberries and sugar in a bowl; mash berries slightly with a fork. Chill, covered, stirring occasionally, for 1 hour.

To make the biscuits, sift dry ingredients; cut in shortening until all ingredients leave the sides of bowl. Drop dough in 8 mounds on buttered baking sheet. Bake in 400 degree oven 20 minutes or until golden brown.

Split each biscuit while slightly warm; spoon strawberries and liquid over bottom half. Put on top half of biscuit; add more berries.

Optional: Ice cream can be added in the middle and the top can have a dollop of whipped cream.

The Fourth of July

We must have Strawberry Shortcake. It is a Fourth of July tradition that no one wants to forget. I have often wondered why Mother's shortcake tasted so good. I believe the reason is because she made it this way using buttermilk.

The Fourth of July

If you have to cook your own chicken, here is an easy and tasty way to do it.

Barbecue Chicken

1 chicken
1 bottle barbecue sauce
1 (10 oz.) bottle 7 Up

Cut chicken into desired pieces and place in skillet. Add salt and pepper to taste. Pour barbecue sauce and 7 Up over chicken. Simmer on top of stove for 1 hour, covered.

Cherry Salad

Remove stones from 2 cups cherries.

Add:

1 C. chopped walnut meats
1 C. chopped celery
3/4 C. mayonnaise

Chill. Arrange in lettuce cups; garnish with one whole cherry.

Joyce's Cherry Breeze

Mix 1 C. cornflake crumbs with 1/3 C. melted butter. Press into a 9" pie pan. Then mix together:

1 pkg. (8 oz.) cream cheese, softened
1 C. sweetened condensed milk
1/2 C. lemon juice
1 t. vanilla

Beat well until smooth; pour in pie shell. Top with one can cherry pie filling. Chill. Serve with a dab of whipped topping if you must.

Cherries

I feel "akin" to the cherry. At an early age I was climbing cherry trees and usually picked enough for my birthday pie. So, naturally, I like to honor our fabulous and versatile cherry. Let's start with a cherry salad from an old cook book published in 1912.

Here is a cool dessert to make on a warm summer's day.

Cherries

To make your own pie filling, do it this way:

Let's not forget that old-time favorite from my friend, Anne Jenkins.

Pie Filling

2 C. fresh pitted cherries

1 C. sugar

2 T. flour (or cornstarch)

1 T. butter

1/2 t. cinnamon

Mix all ingredients, cook until thick and clear.

Cherry Crisp

1 C. flour

1/2 C. rolled oats

1 C. brown sugar

1/2 C. butter or margarine

1 can Cherry Pie Filling

Mix flour and sugar, cut in butter or margarine. Add oats and mix well. Spread half of mixture in 8" square pan; pour pie filling over it. Sprinkle with remaining crumb mixture. Bake 350 degree oven 40 to 45 minutes or until bubbly in the center and golden brown.

Quick Cherry Pie

One baked pie shell (you can buy good ones all ready to bake)
1 C. sugar
1/4 C. cornstarch
1/8 t. salt
2 cans pitted red cherries, drained
1/2 t. almond extract
1/3 C. sliced almonds

Blend sugar, cornstarch and salt in medium bowl; stir in cherries. Microwave on high until mixture is translucent, 8 to 11 minutes, stirring once or twice. Stir in almond extract; pour into baked pie shell. Sprinkle with sliced almonds; chill.

Quick Cherry Sauce

1 can (17 oz.) pitted dark sweet cherries
1 T. cornstarch*
1-1/2 t. lemon juice
1 t. lemon peel, grated

Drain cherries; pour juice into 1-quart bowl, blend in cornstarch until smooth. Microwave on high until clear and thickened, 2-1/2 to 4 minutes, stirring once while cooking. Stir in cherries, lemon juice and peel. Microwave on high until sauce bubbles and cherries are hot, 1-2 minutes. Serve hot or cold.

*Add an additional teaspoon of cornstarch for thicker sauce.

Cherries

My son-in-law, Don, sent me the next two recipes. He loves to experiment with his kitchen equipment. The following are easy, quick and delicious using the microwave.

This is wonderful poured over ice cream, pound cake or any dessert. Imagine this sauce poured over Belgian waffles.

Cherries

This next recipe is deliciously low in calories.
From Deni Hooper.

Lo-Cal Angel Food Cake

1 pkg. Angel Food cake mix
1/2 C. cherries from cherry pie filling, chopped and <u>drained</u>
A bit of almond flavoring

Mix cake according to directions on package. Add cherries and flavoring. Bake according to package directions. Frost cake with confectioner's sugar frosting. Sprinkle with toasted almonds.

Save any leftover pie filling to cover your next cheesecake.

Poached Eggs and Artichoke Hearts

Artichoke hearts—canned or frozen
Fresh or frozen spinach
Hollandaise sauce

If using canned hearts, just heat them thoroughly in a saucepan or microwave. If frozen, cook according to the directions on the package. I used two hearts per person; however, I believe that one heart cut horizontally would be just as tasty and you will get six servings from one can.

Cook the spinach according to directions on package or until tender. Poach the eggs in salted water in a no-stick skillet. Put 2 hearts per person on individual plates; with a slotted spoon put poached eggs on hearts, pour the Hollandaise sauce over eggs and surround with the cooked, drained spinach. This makes a very attractive dish.

Thanks to Mr. L.H. Orebaugh for this easy:

Easy Hollandaise Sauce

3/4 C. mayonnaise
1/3 C. milk
1/4 t. salt
Dash of white pepper
1 T. lemon juice
1 t. grated lemon rind

Blend mayonnaise, milk, salt and pepper in a small saucepan. Heat very slowly, stirring with a wire whisk until smooth. Do not boil. Stir in lemon juice and rind.

Eggs and Salads

Pamper the family with eggs and salads these warm summer days. As many are limiting themselves to just so many eggs a week in order to cut down on cholesterol, I like to make the best use of those precious eggs in recipes that are special to me and my friends. I made this next one recently and served it to two of my severest critics. They loved it.

Serve with cooked artichokes, asparagus, broccoli or poached fish. Also good on Eggs Benedict.

Eggs and Salads

Another special is this:

Our Grandmothers made their own dressings for salads. This is the kind that Mother made.

Shrimp Scrambled Eggs

For about 6 servings use:
8 eggs
1 (11 oz.) can condensed cream of shrimp soup
1 (3-1/2 oz.) can shrimp, drained
1 (4-1/2 oz.) can mushroom pieces, drained
2 T. chopped green onion
1 T. dried parsley flakes
1/4 t. salt
1/4 t. pepper

Beat the eggs and stir in all of the remaining ingredients. Using as little margarine as possible, cook in a non-stick skillet until cooked but not dry, stirring often. Serve hot.

Boiled Cream Dressing

1/4 C. butter
1 t. salt
1 t. mustard
1 t. paprika
3 egg yolks
2 T. flour
1/4 C. vinegar
1 C. cream

Melt butter, add flour and seasonings, eggs and vinegar. Cook until thick; add beaten cream. Beat well; chill and serve. Great for potato, lettuce or cabbage salad.

English Pea Salad

1 can (17 oz.) small early peas
1 jar (12 oz.) pimiento, chopped
1/4 lb. sharp Cheddar cheese, grated
1 small bunch celery hearts, sliced
1 t. sugar
1 t. salt
1 t. red pepper
1 t. chopped onion
Mayonnaise to moisten

Drain peas thoroughly; mix with other ingredients lightly. Chill and serve.

Tomato Soup Salad Dressing

1 small onion, chopped if using blender
1 clove garlic, minced if using blender
1 can tomato soup
3/4 C. vinegar
1/2 to 1 C. sugar
1 t. prepared mustard
1 t. salt
1/2 t. pepper
1 T. Worcestershire sauce
1-1/2 C. salad oil
3 whole cloves

Mince onion and garlic in food processor with metal blade; add soup, vinegar, sugar and seasonings. Slowly add oil with processor running. Pour into quart jar; add cloves and store in refrigerator.

Eggs and Salads

A salad like this one will keep well in the refrigerator for several days; it is great for those who cook for one or two.

"This recipe is an oldie, no one seems to tire of it," says Bette Herbig of Hilton Head, South Carolina. Make it the modern way in a food processor or blender.

Sweet Corn

It seems that our world is without boundaries when we think of the grains in our diet. Though maize or corn as we know it today is the only important grain of American origin and is number one in production worldwide. In the "Good Old Summertime" we think corn on the cob, sweet corn or just green corn. We never thought that there would be a new recipe for corn on the cob. This one sounds great to me.

Roasting Ears with Bacon Butter

Remove all husks and silk; soak ears in cold water. Drain. Spread each ear generously with soft bacon butter*. Wrap in foil, seal tightly. Roast on grill 30 minutes, turning occasionally.

*Bacon Butter

Crumble a few slices of crisp cooked bacon; mix with softened butter or margarine.

You can make this butter ahead of time to keep in the refrigerator for buttering corn prepared another way, or for other vegetables.

Corn Cheese Pudding

From Nony Irey, Pawcotuck, Connecticut

6 ears of corn (3 C. kernels)
4 eggs
1/2 C. finely chopped onion, sauteed
1/2 C. finely chopped green pepper, sauteed
1-1/2 C. milk
1 C. grated Cheddar cheese
1-1/2 C. soft bread crumbs
1 t. salt
1 t. pepper

Preheat oven to 350 degrees. Beat eggs in mixing bowl. Add corn, onion, green pepper, milk, and cheese. Beat. Stir in crumbs, salt and pepper. Transfer to a baking dish. Cover and bake for 30 minutes, then uncover and bake for 15 minutes or until nicely browned and set. Serve warm. Also good cold.

Sweet Corn

I like this famous old-time recipe for Corn Cheese Pudding:

From Our Gardens

Our meal planning and good nutrition comes easy in the summertime. Our farmers' markets are tempting us with beautiful veggies and fruits. I like to stop at those markets especially if I can buy a piece of cherry pie and a cup of coffee. Fresh garden vegetables require very little cooking and are so easy to prepare.

Let's start with a recipe for lemon sauce that is delicious on so many vegetables: The leafy greens, broccoli, zucchini and green and yellow beans.

Lemon Sauce for Vegetables

1 T. cornstarch
1/4 t. salt
1/8 t. pepper
3/4 C. milk
1 T. margarine
1 to 2 T. lemon juice
1 T. chopped parsley

Stir cornstarch, salt and pepper together in 1-quart saucepan. Gradually stir in milk until smooth; add margarine, stirring constantly. Bring to boil over medium heat, boil 1 minute. Remove from heat, stir in lemon juice. Here you can taste to see if you need the second tablespoon of lemon juice. Add parsley; serve over cooked vegetables.

Tomato Medley

3 T. vegetable oil
2 large onions cut in eighths
2 large green peppers, cut into eighths
4 firm tomatoes, cut into eighths
1 T. brown sugar
1 T. cornstarch
1 T. soy sauce
1/2 C. water

Heat oil in skillet over medium heat; add onion. Saute 5 minutes, stirring frequently. Add green peppers and tomatoes.

Combine brown sugar and cornstarch; stir in soy sauce and water. Add mixture to skillet; cook until thickened, stirring constantly. Cover; cook until vegetables are crisp-tender, stirring occasionally.

My Zucchini Stir-Fry

Choose your own ingredients and the amount that you will need for the number of people you are feeding. I used thinly sliced new red potatoes, scrubbed but not peeled; about the same amount of sliced onions (or a little less); a couple of thinly sliced young carrots; 1 tomato, chopped; a little soy sauce, salt and pepper to taste; Sloppy Joe mixture or a bit of spaghetti sauce—whatever you might have already cooked. With one small zucchini, sliced.

Fry potatoes, onions and carrots 2 minutes in a little vegetable oil; add the zucchini and cook another 2 minutes. Add tomatoes, sloppy joe mixture, soy sauce, salt and pepper. to taste; then cook until barely tender. Do not overcook.

From Our Gardens

As soon as home grown tomatoes are ripe, we can make this colorful and tasty serving for six. So easy to prepare.

Our fast growing zucchini is the perfect vegetable for stir-fries. It cooks so quickly, blends with other ingredients, is tasty and adds a beautiful touch of color.

The other day as I was wondering what to have for my supper, when my friend, Phylis, brought me a couple of nice sized zucchini and I decided on a stir-fry. When I was about one half way through it, my friend, Amy, came with a sample of Sloppy Joe mixture that she had just made. So it went into the stir-fry. The result was delicious.

From Our Gardens

Add chunks of zucchini to your next tossed salad; you'll be glad you did. Now is the time to give you Marge Behling's Zucchini Bread

Be sure to pick those fast growing squashes in your garden before they get too big. I found tiny, very young patty pan and summer squash. Janet Dobrowolski told me how to cook them.

Marge Behling's Zucchini Bread

Mix:

3 eggs, beaten
1 C. vegetable oil
2 C. sugar
2 C. grated zucchini

Then add, mixed together:

2 C. flour
1/4 t. baking powder
2 t. baking soda
1 t. salt
1 T. cinnamon

Then add 2 teaspoons vanilla and one cup chopped nuts (optional). Bake in 2 greased loaf pans 1 hour at 250 degrees.

This is rich enough to be considered a dessert. Great to have made ahead of time these warm summer days.

Steamed Baby Summer Squash

Melt a little butter or margarine in a skillet, add a few slices of onion (green onions would be good) and cook them a little. Do not brown. Then add the squash, whole. Cover the pan and steam 3 minutes, you might need to add a very small amount of water to steam them. Season them with salt and pepper at the table. These squash are picked when they are about 1 inch or less in size and so tender.

Janet raises these baby squashes and sells them at our local Farm market; 1 pint will serve 2.

Iced Tea

Make a pot of fresh tea by pouring boiling water over the number of tea bags you need. I use one or two bags for a small pint sized teapot, just enough for myself and a friend. While the tea is steeping, fill tall glasses with ice cubes and pick a sprig of fresh mint.

We are also making iced tea by pouring sun tea over glasses of ice cubes, served with lemon slices and cubes of sugar on the side. I expect that we will have enough hot summer days to enjoy sun tea out on the porch or patio. I guess that everyone knows how to make sun tea, but if you've forgotten, here are the easy directions:

Sun Tea

Place 4 tea bags in a two-quart glass container of cold water; cover and leave in the sun for several hours. This tea never has a bitter taste.

Summer Beverages

Our children are getting their summer liquids from all kinds of containers—boxes, cans, bottles—and there are always fruit juices in the refrigerator. I wonder, sometimes, if they drink water. Iced tea, lemonade, cider, ginger ale floats and ice cream sodas were our specialties during my young years. Iced tea (we called it cold tea) is still a summer favorite. I like to make it this way.

Everyone should have a small plot of mint. I think that nothing makes an iced drink icier than fresh mint. Try it with lemonade.

Summer Beverages

If you want a delicious punch for that family reunion or any summer party, try this. "A pleasant not too sweet punch" from Dot Dolby in "Islanders Cook For Company."

Then there are mint juleps and mint juleps— no two recipes are exactly alike and many experts think that theirs is the only perfect one. Here is one from "Charleston Receipts," published in 1950.

Plantation Punch

1 can (46 oz.) grapefruit juice
1 can (46 oz.) pineapple juice
1 quart ginger ale
1/2 gallon pineapple sherbet

Chill juices and ginger ale in refrigerator at least 8 hours before serving. Just before serving, combine juices and ginger ale; add sherbet cut in at least 6 pieces. Makes 35 servings

Mint Julep

For each cold goblet use:
Several mint leaves
2 to 3 t. sugar syrup*
Crushed ice
1 oz. bourbon
1 sprig of mint

Crush leaves; let stand in syrup. Put syrup into a cold silver julep cup or glass; add ice, which has been crushed and rolled in a towel to dry. Pour in whiskey; stir, not touching the glass. Add sprig of mint; serve immediately.

*Sugar syrup: Make it this way: use about an equal amount of water and sugar, stirring until sugar dissolves.

Refrigerator Bread and Butter Pickles

1 gallon cucumbers, sliced and mixed with sliced onions, using about 1/4 as many onions as cucumbers.

1/2 C. salt
4 C. vinegar
4 C. sugar
1-1/2 t. celery seed
1-1/2 T. mustard seed
1-1/2 T. tumeric

Sprinkle cucumbers and onions with the 1/2 cup salt; cover with ice cubes. Let set 2 to 4 hours; drain.

Bring remaining ingredients to a boil; cool. Pour over cucumbers and onions; put in large jar or quart cans. Keep in refrigerator. These pickles are so good, they will not last long. In fact they are really good after several months in the refrigerator.

It's Pickling Time

About this time of the year many of us are "in a pickle" trying to decide whether to make pickles or not like Grandmother used to do. On the negative side we do not have the equipment in our kitchens that Grandmother had, such as crocks, barrels, big kettles and a cellar to keep them in for months. On the positive side, we do have refrigerators, freezers and canners. We are pickling, though with a different style. The following recipe is a universal favorite. Have this recipe handy for:

It's Pickling Time

Here is a long-time tried-and-true recipe from the Ball Company. A pot roast of beef is out of this world when you pour this sauce over the top while roasting it.

Spicy Chili Sauce

4 quarts peeled, cored, chopped ripe tomatoes (24)
1-1/2 C. chopped green peppers (3 medium)
2 C. chopped onions
1-1/2 C. vinegar
1-1/2 C. sugar
1 T. salt
1 t. ground ginger
1 t. ground cinnamon
1 t. ground allspice
1 t. ground cloves
1 T. celery seed

Combine all ingredients; simmer until thick as desired, 1-1/2 hours, stirring frequently to prevent burning or sticking. Pour boiling sauce in hot canning jars, leaving 1/4 inch head space; process 15 minutes in water bath canner. Makes 8 pints.

Note: Chili sauce is not a bright red color because ground spices are used.

Pickled Wax Beans

We find delicious relishes on our grocers' shelves.

1 can (16 ozs.) wax beans or steamed ones from the garden
1/4 C. pickle relish
1 T. butter or margarine

Heat beans, drain. Toss with relish and butter. Serve hot.

Quick Corn Relish

1 can whole kernel corn
2 T. onion flakes
2 t. celery seed
1/3 C. sugar
1/3 C. vinegar
1/3 C. sweet pickle relish
1/3 C. diced pimientos

Combine 1/4 C. liquid drained from corn and the drained corn with remaining ingredients; simmer 10 minutes. Serve hot or cold. Makes 2-1/2 cups.

It's Pickling Time

Here is a delicious way to spice up wax beans anytime through the year.

If you want some quick relish, do it this way:

Harvest

Harvest was a busy time on our family farm; the oats and wheat were stacked in the fields. It was time for the big, noisy and smoky steam engine to haul the threshing machine from one farm to the next, the neighborhood men following with their teams to bring in the grain. It was a holiday time for us as children; we loved the excitement.

Mother had been working from "Dawn 'til dark" preparing enough food for those hungry men. She never heard of a forty hour week. The early harvest apples ripened at this same time so there was always apple pie on the thresher's table. These early apples make perfect pie and applesauce. This next recipe would have been welcomed by Mother although pizza was not a part of our vocabulary in those days.

Apple Pizza

1/4 C. flour
1 t. salt
1/2 C. shortening
1 C. shredded Cheddar cheese
1/2 C. ice water
1/2 C. powdered non-dairy cream or powdered milk
1/2 C. brown sugar
1/2 C. white sugar
1/3 C. flour
1 t. cinnamon
1/2 t. nutmeg
1/4 t. salt
1/4 C. butter
6 C. peeled apples, 1/2 inch slices
2 T. lemon juice

Mix flour and salt together; cut in shortening. Add cheese; mix well. Sprinkle in ice water; form into a ball. Roll out; press on 15 inch pizza pan and press up edges for a rim.

Combine powdered cream or milk, brown and white sugars, flour, cinnamon, nutmeg and salt together; sprinkle 1/2 of mixture on crust. Arrange apple slices in circles to cover crust; sprinkle with lemon juice. Cut butter into remaining mixture and cover apples. Bake in 450 degree oven until apples are tender. Serve warm, plain or with ice cream.

Canned Peaches

Be sure to follow the directions in your canner book. It tells exactly how to do it. Peaches, tomatoes and all kinds of berries and fruits can be canned in the hot water bath. My directions for peaches states: Wash, remove skins and pit, drain and place in jars: For cold pack, cover with boiling syrup (thin or medium), process in hot water bath 25 minutes for pints and 30 minutes for quarts. For hot pack, process only 10 minutes for pints and 15 minutes for quarts.

Here is a recipe for syrup; sugar helps canned fruit hold its shape, color and flavor.

Syrup for Canning

To two cups of water or juice, add 2 cups of sugar for 5 cups of thin syrup; add 3 cups of sugar for 5 cups of medium syrup and 4-3/4 cups of sugar for heavy syrup. Bring to a boil and pour over fruit in cans.

Peach Crumble

4 C. peaches—fresh, canned or frozen
1 C. flour
1 C. brown sugar
1/4 C. butter

Arrange peach slices in greased 8 inch baking dish. Blend flour and sugar; cut in butter. This mixture will be crumbly. Sprinkle crumb mixture over peaches. Bake in 375 degree oven 30 minutes. Delicious with ice cream.

Harvest

Soon after the grain is harvested it is time to can peaches. It still seems that no commercial peaches can quite produce that special flavor of the home canned variety.

While peaches are ripe you will want to make this easy dessert:

Barbecues

According to an Indian legend, corn, beans and squash are "Loving sisters who must always be planted together." I admire their philosophy, which includes all nature in a loving way, and I can almost see Indian children playing around the campfire while their mothers were cooking supper. It seems that our barbecues are as in-tune with nature as were those campfires of our original Americans.

Let's face it—hot dogs are an American barbecue favorite. We like to smother them with our own fixings, so let us have onions, catsup, mustard and relish handy. However, if we want to fancy them up a bit, try this variation.

Franks Italiano

1 lb. jumbo franks or jumbo beef franks
1 medium tomato, peeled, chopped and drained
3 T. grated American cheese
3 T. Parmesan cheese
1 small clove garlic, minced
1/4 t. crushed oregano
8 slices bacon
8 hot dog buns

Partially split franks lengthwise, cutting almost to ends. Combine tomato, cheeses, garlic and oregano; stuff into frank. Wrap a bacon slice around each frank, anchoring ends with wooden toothpicks. Place franks on grill; cook over hot coals, turning often, 10 to 15 minutes or until filling is hot and bacon is crisp.

Herbed Chicken

3/4 C. salad dressing (Ranch or Italian is good)
1/2 C. chicken broth
2 cloves garlic, minced
2 T. finely chopped green onions
2 t. crushed basil
6 halves boneless chicken breasts, skin removed

Mix dressing, chicken broth, garlic, onions and seasonings; pour mixture over chicken. Cover, refrigerate several hours or overnight. Drain. Place chicken on grill over medium-hot coals (coals will have a slight glow) or rack of your broiler pan; grill or broil 8-10 minutes on each side or until tender.

Potatoes in Foil

Thinly slice as many scrubbed new potatoes as needed and a few green onions. Put one serving of potatoes and a few green onions on individual squares of foil. Sprinkle with Italian dressing. Wrap foil tightly, bake on grill over medium-hot coals until potatoes are tender. Check after 15 to 20 minutes; grill a little longer if necessary. Everyone has his own serving and the foil makes its own serving dish—another way to save dishwashing. These delicious potatoes can be made in the microwave using plastic wrap in place of foil.

Barbecues

Another favorite is chicken.

Picnics

It's a good idea to be prepared for any kind of weather when planning a picnic. Always have a rain-proof jacket or sweater along. One sweltering, hot summer afternoon Shirley and I decided to do some sun bathing on the sand dunes north of Cross Village. We packed a light lunch with some cool drinks and settled down in the warm sand. Then there was suddenly a cold blast of air; I think that it came across Lake Michigan directly from the North Pole. We hurriedly donned our slacks and sweaters and rushed to the car, ending up at the Fort at Mackinaw City huddled around a fireplace where a lady was demonstrating the spinning wheel, then to a fast food place for a warm sandwich. Picnics like this become enduring treasures.

Here is a new taste in hamburgers if you are going to have a fire.

Korean Beef Patties

It is better if you can prepare the patties before leaving home. Wrap in foil or plastic on ice and cook them at your favorite picnic spot. Be sure to put some extra green onions in your basket.

1 lb. ground beef
4 T. soy sauce
2 T. sugar
1 T. sesame seeds, crushed
2-1/2 T. chopped green onions
1 T. garlic, minced
Dash of black pepper

Combine all ingredients. Form into four balls; flatten into patties. Broil, grill or panfry until done. 4 servings.

Vegetable Dip

2 hard boiled eggs
4 garlic buds—go by your own taste here and the size of the buds
2 T. horseradish
1 T. paprika
1 t. salt
1 pint mayonnaise, not salad dressing
2 T. olive oil
2 T. vinegar

Blend all ingredients together in blender; chill.

Picnic Pasta Salad

8 oz. uncooked macaroni, any style
8 oz. Italian dressing
1 T. Dijon-style mustard
1/4 t. black pepper
2 C. assorted frozen vegetables, thawed and drained
1 medium red or green pepper
1/2 C. sliced ripe olives
2 T. chopped fresh parsley

Cook macaroni according to package directions; drain and rinse with cold water until completely cool. Blend Italian dressing, mustard and pepper in large bowl; stir in vegetables, red and green pepper, olives and parsley. Add macaroni; toss well. Cover; chill at least 2 hours.

Picnics

Fix some veggies ahead of time and store in a plastic bag with some ice. Here is a tasty dip:

For that family reunion or club picnic we do a little extra fixing. This salad is delicious and sort of replaces the old-fashioned potato salad.

63

Pies

We know that apple pie was a staple food during early colonial days, often served with a slab of cheese, and has continued to be America's favorite. This is the way that Mother made her pie.

Later in the Fall and through the winter, Mother made her delicious apple pies with Northern Spy apples. Many good cooks have told me that they are the perfect apple for pie.

Mother's Apple Pie

She made her own tender flaky crust using lard for shortening. Now, I buy a good quality double crust from the frozen or dairy sections of the supermarket. They are good; follow the directions on the packages. In summer Mother used the early harvest apples, slicing enough to generously fill a pie crust.

First sprinkle a little flour on bottom crust and spread about 1/4 cup sugar, then add the sliced apples. Then add 3/4 cups sugar to apples and sprinkle lightly with cinnamon and flour. Dab lots of butter over all. Cover with top crust. Cut slits in top for steam to escape.

Bake 15 minutes at 400 degrees, then lower heat to 325 degrees until apples are tender and crust is a golden brown. Good warm or cold. Mother often served her pie with whipped cream.

No-Bake
Peach Melba Pie

Line a buttered 9-inch pie pan with whole vanilla wafers; chill 30 minutes. Dissolve 1 package lemon flavored gelatin in 1-1/4 cups hot water; add one package (10 oz.) frozen raspberries and 1 package (12 oz.) frozen peaches. Separate fruit with a fork; chill until partially congealed. Pour into cookie pie shell; chill until firm. Top with whipped topping; garnish with berries.

Pies

On a hot day when no one wants to use the oven, we can make a gorgeous pie with a no-bake crust. It makes a lovely summer dessert.

Fall

Table of Contents

Fall

Green Tomato Pie

3 C. chopped green tomatoes
2 C. raisins, soaked and drained
1-1/2 C. brown sugar
1 t. cinnamon
1/2 t. nutmeg (optional)
1/4 t. salt
7 T. lemon juice
4 T. butter
3-1/2 T. flour

Combine sugar, flour, salt, lemon juice, spices, raisins and tomatoes. Line a 9-inch pie pan with pastry; pour in filling. Dot with butter; cover with top crust. Bake in 450 degree oven 10 minutes; reduce heat to 350 and bake 45 minutes, or until tomatoes are tender.

Tomatoes

How can I express my appreciation for our beautiful Autumn days in Northern Michigan? On the first day of Fall I notice that many of my friends are making ready to migrate south and already some of my favorite birds have already left for warmer climates. Personally, I do not feel that urge; I tell myself that we have at least six good weeks to explore and enjoy our beautiful North Country.

The harvest is abundant and from our kitchens emanates the aroma of preserves, jellies and pickles. Up until the time that we have a black frost we will have ripe tomatoes in our gardens and we will be making use of those green ones that will not have had time to ripen. Here is an old-time favorite from Esther Welch.

Tomatoes

My taste buds seem to remember just how much I loved this Chow Chow that Mother also made with green tomatoes.

Grandmother served her sliced ripe tomatoes in a pretty dish with a vinegar cruet handy, also sugar, salt and pepper to use as we wished. Now, I like to serve them with either celery seed or poppy seed dressing.

Another delicious oldie is:

Mother's Chow Chow

19 large green tomatoes
7 large green apples
7 large onions
7 C. vinegar
7 C. sugar
2 t. allspice
2 t. cinnamon
2 t. cloves
1 t. black pepper

Slice tomatoes, lay in salt water overnight. Chop all ingredients together; add spices. Boil 4 hours, slowly. The old recipe does not say how to go on from there. I would seal them in pint jars and put them in a hot water bath for at least 5 minutes to seal properly.

Sauteed Green Tomatoes

Slice green tomatoes, season with salt and pepper. Dip in dry fine bread crumbs (fine cracker crumbs can also be used), beaten egg and then in the crumbs again. Saute in hot dry pan with a little oil or butter. Serve on buttered toast.

Pear Grape Salad

4 ripe dessert pears
1 C. cream cheese
1 to 2 T. French dressing
1/2 lb. black grapes
Crisp lettuce, optional

Peel pears; cut in half. Scoop out core with teaspoon. Blend cream cheese with enough French dressing to make spreadable; coat rounded side of each pear half. Place on platter, cut side down. Halve and seed grapes; press into cheese close together so each pear resembles a small bunch of grapes. Decorate with lettuce or mint leaves if you wish.

Pears in Chocolate Sauce

1 can (29 ozs.) pear halves

Chocolate Sauce:
8 ozs. semi-sweet chocolate
2 T. hot water
1 T. butter
1 egg yolk
1/2 C. heavy cream
1 egg white
Chopped pistachio nuts, for garnish

Drain pears; arrange in 6 individual serving dishes. Place chocolate in top of double boiler; stir in water. Melt chocolate over boiling water; remove from heat. Add butter, stirring until melted. Add egg yolk and cream. Before serving, beat egg white until stiff peaks form, fold in warm chocolate sauce. Spoon over pears. Sprinkle with chopped pistachio nuts, if desired.

Pears

Pears nearly always need to be picked green because they spoil easily after ripening. They keep well as long as they are refrigerated, so they are available all year, though they are at their best from August through December. Ripen them a few days at room temperature, then refrigerate and use within 3 to 5 days.

Serve them in thick slices with your favorite cheese for a delicious dessert. The old-timers served pears peeled and thinly sliced with a little brown sugar and fresh cream—a dessert to remember. Here are a few suggestions on how to use and enjoy this delicious fruit.

Pears

Your family and guests will love this:

Pears with Raspberry Sauce

4 large fresh pears
3 C. water
1 cinnamon stick
2 whole cloves
2 inch piece of lemon peel
3 T. honey
6 T. cottage cheese
1 T. lemon juice
1 pkg. (10 oz.) frozen whole raspberries
4 t. sliced almonds

Peel pears, cut in half, carefully remove cores. Combine water, cinnamon, cloves, lemon peel and 2 tablespoons of honey in a saucepan; bring to boil. Add pears; simmer 10 minutes. Remove pears with slotted spoon; drain. Puree cottage cheese in blender; spoon into bowl. Stir in lemon juice and 1 tablespoon honey, adjusting sweetness to taste.

Fill pear halves with cottage cheese mixture. Puree raspberries, reserving a few for garnish. Pour over pears in a pretty bowl or individual dessert dishes. Garnish with whole berries or almonds if you wish.

Half-hour Apple Butter

2 C. unsweetened applesauce, homemade or purchased
1/4 to 1/2 C. sugar
1 t. cinnamon
1/4 t. allspice
1/8 t. each ginger and cloves

Combine all ingredients in a 1-1/2 quart heavy saucepan. Bring to boil; cook 30 minutes, stirring often. Makes 1-1/4 cups.

Homemade Applesauce

Don't forget to make homemade applesauce with those crispy fresh apples. Peel, quarter and core them and cook in a very little water until tender; stirring often. Mash them a bit but leave a few small chunks. Season with cinnamon and sugar to taste. Serve warm with pancakes one of these cool nights. Now is the time when apples taste their very best.

Apple Days

Down memory lane I can almost taste the tangy air in our old orchard. This was the time of the year when we took enough apples to the cider mill for two barrels of cider and Mother had a large kettle of sweet apples cooking in cider on the back of the stove.

Even though I cook for one and have a few guests only on occasion, I have the urge to preserve the luscious Fall fruits; even to make apple butter. It just happens that I have an old newspaper clipping with a recipe for those who might want a wee bit of old-time flavor.

Apple Days

Sometimes I wonder if there could be another apple recipe. Then Maryanne Halstad of Zerring, Iowa gave me this one. It's like a glorified cobbler.

Frozen Applesauce

If you want your applesauce cold, just freeze it. When you are ready for some, partially thaw it for a delicious dessert. Add a dab of cream topping or a scoop of ice cream for a delightful dish any day of the year. The apple sauce can be thawed in the microwave as a last minute treat when friends drop in.

Apple Joy

Make a biscuit dough from a mix (use recipe using 2 cups of mix)

4 apples, chopped

Roll out dough like a jelly roll. Cover with chopped apples. Roll up and cut off in one-inch slices, place close together in buttered pan. Sprinkle generously with brown sugar and cinnamon.

Then mix together:
1 C. sugar
1 T. flour
1 T. butter
1 C. hot water

Cook for 2 minutes. Pour over pudding. Bake 375 degrees about 30 minutes or until apples are tender and lightly browned. Serve with whipped topping.

Colcannon

Potatoes
Cabbage
Butter or drippings
Salt and pepper

Take equal amounts of boiled potatoes and boiled cabbage. Mash the potatoes and mince the cabbage. Melt a piece of butter or drippings in a saucepan, allowing about one ounce to the pound of vegetables. Put in the potatoes and cabbage and add salt and pepper to taste. Mix well.

Heat thoroughly and serve or turn into a greased pie dish, sprinkle with grated cheese, dot with butter or margarine, and brown in a hot oven.

Halloween

Last night my friend, Amy, and I went for an early evening walk. The magic of the shortening days was upon us. Already the color was gone from the trees and we walked through crisp dry leaves. It is easy to understand the awe and fear that our long-ago ancestors felt when the leaves left the trees and their weird shapes were revealed in a darkening sky. They built bonfires to frighten the spirits away. The magic is still there and it is easy to understand why we have Halloween; it is almost an instinct. I am happy now to see that Halloween is a fun time, especially for the children.

It's party time; we must have cider and doughnuts, they have already become a tradition as well as popcorn and apples. Here is an age-old recipe which has been served and still is prepared in Ireland, Scotland and Northern England. Cabbage, apples and nuts played an important role in ancient Halloween feasts.

Halloween

Our children still love cookies and brownies like Grandma made.

Oatmeal Cookies

1 C. brown sugar
1 C. white sugar
1/2 lb. butter or margarine
2 eggs
1 C. oatmeal
1 C. coconut
1 t. baking powder
1 t. soda
1/4 t. salt
6 oz. butterscotch chips, if desired

Cream together the sugars, butter or margarine and eggs. Measure and mix together all dry ingredients and add to creamed mixture. Mix well. Add butterscotch chips if desired. Shape balls of dough the size of walnuts and place on baking sheet, do not press down. Bake at 350 degrees until lightly browned.

Brownies

3/4 C. flour
1/2 C. cocoa
1/4 t. baking powder
1/4 t. salt
1 C. sugar
1/3 C. butter, softened
2 eggs
1 t. vanilla
3/4 C. coarsely chopped walnuts

Preheat oven to 350 degrees.

In large bowl, combine sugar, butter, eggs and vanilla; beat until creamy.

In small bowl, combine flour, cocoa, baking powder and salt. Gradually blend the flour mixture into the creamy one, stir in nuts. Pour into greased 8 inch square baking pan. Bake at 350 degrees for 20 to 25 minutes. Cool completely, cut into 2" squares.

Happy Halloween.

Halloween

A good beginner's recipe for young cooks and a favorite of all kids from nine to ninety!

It's Nutting Time

American Indians appreciated the food value of nuts and they gathered them in large quantities. When the pioneers were clearing their land, they left the promising nut trees. Nuts provided a way of socializing for our pioneers. They collected them during autumn days with friends and cracked them around the open fireplace during long winter evenings.

Grandma made good use of those nuts. Nut cake recipes kept cropping up in the old cookbooks.

I love this sinfully delicious rich cake:

Praline Cake With Brown Sugar Topping

1/2 C. butter or margarine, softened

2 C. firmly packed brown sugar

2 eggs

2 C. all purpose flour

2 T. cocoa

1 t. soda

1/4 t. salt

1 C. buttermilk

1 t. vanilla

Brown Sugar Topping (recipe follows)

Cream butter; gradually add sugar, beating until light and fluffy. Add eggs, one at a time, beating mixture well after each addition. Combine flour, cocoa, soda and salt; add to creamed mixture alternately with buttermilk, beginning and ending with flour mixture. Stir in vanilla.

Pour batter into greased and floured 13 x 9 x 2 inch baking pan. Bake in 350 degree oven 25 to 30 minutes or until wooden pick inserted in center comes out clean.

Pour Brown Sugar Topping evenly over cake. Broil 5 inches from broiler element for 1 minute. Cool; cut into squares. Leftovers can be frozen.

Brown Sugar Topping

1 C. firmly packed brown sugar
1 C. chopped pecans or walnuts
1/3 C. evaporated milk

Combine all ingredients in saucepan; boil 1 minute, stirring constantly.

Great for that potluck supper.

Nut Fingers

2 C. flour
1-1/2 sticks of butter or margarine
4 T. sugar
1 t. vanilla
1 C. nuts, chopped

Sift flour and sugar into large bowl with butter; blend well with hands. Add vanilla; then add nuts. Using about 1 tablespoon at a time, roll into pieces about the size of a finger. Bake on cookie sheet at 250 degrees about 45 minutes. This is another way to serve scones or shortbread.

It's Nutting Time

Tips on Using Nutmeats

1—When the recipe says "optional," it would be better to use them.
2—For everyday crisp garden salad, add the delicious crunch of nutmeats using almonds, pecans or walnuts
3—Take some along for a picnic on the road
4—For a delicious salad just add pecan halves to lettuce, sliced red onions, sliced mushrooms; you will be glad you did.

This recipe is very similar to Scotch Shortbread.

Hunting Season

Young "Old Sports" Cook Their Trophies

Every year my friend, Al Bostwick, and his cronies take a hunting trip, and usually come home with elk, venison and lots of pictures. I do not know if Al and his friends would appreciate being called "old sports." Yet, according to Stan Perkins of Lore of the Wolverine, "For some unbeknown reason sportsmen have always been referred to as old sports. Young sports seem to be as scarce as cock pheasants on opening day of hunting season."

Al's Roast Venison or Elk

Al cooks his elk and venison the same way, but does not mix the two meats. He wants to retain the special flavor of each separately. (He does cook venison roasts and steaks together and the same for elk steaks and roasts.)

3 to 4 lbs. venison roast and steaks or elk roast and steaks
1 can cream of mushroom soup
1 can cream of celery soup
1 large onion (1 cup) coarsely chopped
1 soup can water
Lawry's seasoned salt

Sear meat in olive oil to brown. Season well with Lawry's seasoned salt and pepper. Put roast in medium size roaster. Combine remaining ingredients; add to roast in pan. If Al is using steaks too, he puts them on top and pours the mixture over all, even putting a little bit of the sauce under the roast. Roast in 350 degree oven 4 to 4-1/2 hours.

After about 3 hours of roasting he checks the juices in the pan, mixing it up. He will leave the cover off the pan for part of the last hour of cooking if there is a lot of liquid. He might add a little water instead of taking the cover from the roast if the meat is dry and sometimes he thickens it to gravy consistency with a little flour and water mixture. There is no fat on these roasts.

Bill's Mucky Duck Barbecued Beans

This amount will feed 24 people, which could be about right for a group of hungry hunters. Bill usually cuts this recipe in half.

2 lb. of bacon strips, cut in thirds
1 large onion, chopped
5 cans pork and beans
1 bottle (24 ozs.) catsup
1 pkg. (16 ozs.) brown sugar
1/4 C. Mucky Duck mustard (from the supermarket)
3/4 C. Worcestershire sauce
1 T. liquid smoke

Fry bacon in 4 to 6 quart pot; drain, leaving enough fat to saute onion. Add remaining ingredients; simmer, uncovered, 1 to 2 hours. Bill used his slow cooker for this, but has also cooked it in a pot on the stove. Both ways are good.

Bill's Venison Swiss Steak

He also used his slow cooker for venison Swiss steak by pounding flour into the steak, browning in skillet and adding 1 can of mushroom soup and 1 can water. Pour into slow cooker, cook several hours.

What a wonderful season this has been. I just received a gift of Great Lakes salmon. Some of the "old sports" were out there fishing.

Hunting Season

Then there is Bill Harris, who loves to bow hunt. He likes to put food in his slow cooker so he has something good to eat when returning from a day in the woods. Here is:

Pork

It's the season for good fresh pork. It still is one of America's favorite meats. We are now eliminating most of its fat in our cooking and farmers are raising hogs with more lean meat. Once again pork has its time-honored place at the top of our menus, like this old-time fall goodie.

Pork Chops and Sauerkraut

2 bags (1 lb. each) fresh sauerkraut, rinsed and drained
1 lb. new potatoes, halved
1 T. oil
4 one-half inch thick pork chops
Salt and pepper
3/4 C. water
1/4 t. salt
1/2 t. pepper
1/2 t. caraway seeds

Heat oil in large stainless steel or non-stick pan over medium-high heat. (Iron or aluminum may react with acidity in sauerkraut and give it an off-flavor and color.)

Sprinkle chops with salt and pepper to taste; brown on both sides, 4 minutes in all. Remove. Put potatoes in same pan, brown cut side, 2 minutes. Remove. Pour in water, scrape up browned bits on pan bottom. Add sauerkraut and rest of ingredients. Lower heat; simmer covered, until chops are very tender, about 40 minutes. Taste for seasoning, add more salt and pepper if needed.

Escalloped Tomatoes

Fill a baking dish with fresh cut bread cubes, then pour stewed or canned tomatoes over them. Add some finely chopped onion and sweeten with a little brown sugar. Season with salt and pepper; dot with butter and bake until bubbly.

Glazed Ham & Raisin Meatballs

1/2 lb. ground ham
1/2 lb. ground fresh pork
1 C. raisin bran flakes
1 can (6 ozs.) evaporated milk (3/4 cup)
1 egg
1 T. finely chopped onion
Dash salt, pepper and crushed dried thyme
1/4 C. brown sugar
1/2 C. corn syrup
1 T. vinegar
1/2 t. dry mustard

Thoroughly mix first 7 ingredients; shape into 8 or 10 meatballs, using about 1/4 C. of mixture for each. Place in 11 x 7 x 1-1/2 inch baking pan. Bake uncovered, in 350 degree oven, 30 minutes.

Combine rest of ingredients in small saucepan; bring to boil. Pour over ham balls; bake 20 minutes, basting with sauce once or twice. Makes 4 to 5 servings.

Pork

Grandma would serve stewed tomatoes this way to accompany this meal:

This recipe will be appreciated by those who like ham with raisin sauce.

Pork

Our family loves:

Bill's Farmers' Country Breakfast

6 ozs. pork sausage (bulk is best)
1-1/2 Southern style hash brown potatoes
1/4 C. chopped onion
6 eggs
1/3 C. milk
1/2 t. salt
1/2 t. parsley flakes (Bill used dill weed)
1 pkg. (4 ozs.) shredded Cheddar cheese

Cook sausage over medium heat in a 10 inch skillet, stirring occasionally until light brown. Remove sausage from pan drippings; add potatoes and onion to drippings; cook over medium heat, stirring occasionally, until potatoes begin to brown 5 to 7 minutes. Reduce heat to medium.

Beat together eggs, milk, salt and parsley; pour over potato mixture. Add sausage; scramble. Top with cheese, cover. Heat until cheese is melted.

Makes 4 generous servings

Cranberry Sauce

2 t. cornstarch
1/4 t. cinnamon
1/8 t. salt
1/2 t. grated orange peel
2 T. orange juice
2 T. dry sherry
1 can (16 oz.) whole cranberry sauce

Mix all ingredients in a small saucepan; cook, stirring often, over medium heat until thickened. Use 1/2 cup of this sauce to glaze your meat while roasting. Serve with remaining sauce.

Thanksgiving—
Triggers kinship with yesterday

What moistens the lips
What brightens the eye
What brings back the past
Like a rich pumpkin pie.

From an old cookbook

We like this kinship with the past; to belong, in a sense, to yesterday. Our minds journey back to the first Thanksgiving feast which introduced the Pilgrims to food gifts from the Indians such as corn, beans, pumpkins, turkey, squash and cranberries.

So it is "fitting" that we cook those traditional foods with thanksgiving. Mother always had a pretty dish of cranberry sauce as a centerpiece at our Thanksgiving table. This recipe is a terrific sauce to glaze turkey, ham, pork roast or Cornish game hens.

Thanksgiving

This next old-time dish using tomatoes and corn is good with any meal.

Escalloped Corn and Tomatoes

2 cans (14 or 16 ozs.) whole tomatoes, drained and cut up
1 can (8 ozs.) whole kernel corn, drained
1 can (8 ozs.) cream style corn
2 eggs, slightly beaten
2 T. flour
2 t. sugar
1/2 t. pepper
1/4 C. butter or margarine
1 medium onion, finely chopped
1 clove garlic, minced
4 C. soft bread crumbs
1/4 C. grated Parmesan cheese

Combine tomatoes, cream style corn, whole kernel corn, eggs, flour, sugar and pepper. Turn into a 12 x 7-1/2 x 2 inch baking pan.

Melt butter or margarine in medium saucepan, add onion and garlic. Cook until onion is tender, but not brown. Combine crumbs and cheese. Add butter mixture to breadcrumb mixture, tossing to combine. Sprinkle over tomato mixture in baking dish. Bake in 350 degree oven 30 minutes or until a knife inserted near the center comes out clean. 8 servings.

Glazed Butternut Squash

2-1/2 lbs. butternut squash, seeded and cut into 1 inch slices, then peeled
1/2 C. packed brown sugar
1/4 C. butter or margarine
1/4 t. paprika
1/2 t. salt

Arrange squash slices in a 11 x 9 x 2 inch pan. Cover, bake in 350 degree oven 1 hour.

Combine brown sugar, butter, paprika and salt in small saucepan. Cook, stirring until mixture is bubbly. Spoon over squash in baking pan. Return to oven, bake uncovered 25 minutes or until squash is tender. 6 to 8 servings.

This can be made ahead of time and reheated.

Thanksgiving

Squash has long graced our Thanksgiving table. This is one of my favorites.

Thanksgiving

Pumpkin pie is traditional; these pumpkin pie bars will give us all the flavor of pumpkin pie in just a different form. They are easy to make and there is no need to roll out a crust.

Pumpkin Pie Squares

1 pkg. yellow cake mix (2 layer size)
1/2 C. melted butter or margarine
3 eggs divided
1 can (16 oz.) pumpkin
1 can evaporated milk (2/3 cup)
1/2 C. packed brown sugar
2-1/2 t. pumpkin pie spice
2 t. sugar
2 T. butter or margarine
1 t. cinnamon
Whipped cream

Combine dry cake mix, melted butter or margarine and 1 egg in large bowl, beating until combined. Reserve 1 cup of mixture. Spread remaining mixture in an ungreased 13 x 9 x 2 inch baking pan to form an even crust.

Filling: Beat remaining 2 eggs, pumpkin, evaporated milk, brown sugar and spice together in medium mixing bowl; pour over prepared crust.

Combine the reserved 1 cup of the cake-mix mixture, 2 teaspoons sugar, butter and cinnamon; dot evenly over pumpkin filling. Bake in 350 degree oven 45-50 minutes. Cool in pan on wire rack. Serve with whipped cream; store in refrigerator. Makes 12 servings.

Happy Thanksgiving!

Turkey Rice Casserole

1-1/2 C. water
1/2 t. salt
2 t. butter or margarine
1-1/2 C. minute rice (uncooked)
2 chicken bouillon cubes
1/2 C. water
1/2 C. milk
1 pkg. (9 oz.) frozen small onions with cream sauce
1 C. sweet green peas
1-1/2 C. diced cold turkey
2 T. sliced black olives (optional)
1 T. butter or margarine (optional)
1/4 C. grated Parmesan cheese

Combine 1-1/2 cups water, salt, 2 teaspoons butter and rice in 1-1/2 quart casserole. Cover and bake at 450 for 10 minutes. Meanwhile, heat bouillon cubes and 1/2 cup water in saucepan until cubes are dissolved. Add milk, onions, peas, turkey, olives, and 1 tablespoon butter. Cook and simmer about 4 minutes.

Move rice to edge of casserole; pour turkey into center. Sprinkle with parmesan cheese. Place in preheated broiler for 2 to 3 minutes until lightly browned. 4 servings.

Leftovers

Leftovers are no problem any more with the advent of the microwave. In fact, many of us cook large portions of our favorite foods just so we will have leftovers. Complete meals can be heated right on the serving plate and they often taste even better the second time around. There are endless possibilities with leftovers, such as baked squash and stuffing with turkey or chicken slices on individual plates. Then re-heat that mince or apple pie for dessert.

Do you want a leftover recipe, easy to make in 15 to 20 minutes using minute rice and frozen vegetables? This meal has an elegant appearance, putting leftover turkey or chicken in the gourmet class.

Leftovers

I *still like old-fashioned hash. The next recipe is good using roasted meat—beef, pork, corned beef or lamb.*

Savory Meat and Potato Hash

1 T. butter or margarine
1 small onion, diced
1 stalk celery, sliced
1 C. cubed roasted meat—beef, pork, corned beef or lamb
2 med. sized pre-baked potatoes, peeled and cubed
1/2 t. salt (optional)
1/4 t. pepper
1/4 C. leftover gravy (or canned)

Melt margarine or butter in saucepan. Saute onions and celery until tender. Add cubed meat and stir until heated through. Add potatoes and brown slightly. Add seasonings to taste and just enough gravy to moisten. (You can use canned gravy for this if your gravy is all gone.) Makes 2 servings.

Turkey Salad Burritos

2 C. chopped cooked turkey
3/4 C. finely chopped celery
1/2 C. finely chopped onion
1/4 to 1/2 C. sliced black olives
1 C. shredded cheddar cheese
1/2 C. salad dressing or mayonnaise
1/4 c. picante sauce
1/2 t. salt
6 soft flour tortillas (7 to 8 inches)
Picante sauce
Black olives for garnish

In medium mixing bowl, combine turkey, celery, onion, black olives and cheese. In another bowl, whisk together salad dressing, picante sauce and salt. Pour sauce over turkey mixture; blend well. Spoon filling onto tortillas; wrap burrito-style. Heat until thoroughly warmed or microwave each burrito 2 to 2-1/2 minutes on high. Serve with additional picante sauce; garnish with black olives.

Leftovers

This is a new style use for some of that turkey meat. Our younger generation will love these:

Leftovers

Quite often I have cranberry sauce left from our Thanksgiving dinner. This is a good way to enjoy it as a dessert.

Grandmother made a wonderful leftover dessert that many of us still relish, using some of her delicious homemade bread that had become a little dry.

Cranberry Yogurt

3/4 C. whole berry cranberry sauce
2 C. plain yogurt
1/2 C. granola, homemade or purchased

Place about 2 tablespoons cranberry sauce in bottom of 4 parfait glasses. Layer yogurt, remaining cranberry sauce, and granola on top. 4 servings.

Grandmother's Bread Pudding

2 C. scalded milk
2 T. butter
1 C. dried bread, cut in 1/2 inch squares
1 C. shredded coconut
1/3 C. sugar
1/4 t. vanilla
1/2 t. almond extract
2 eggs slightly beaten
1/4 t. salt

Combine milk, butter and bread squares. Add sugar, salt and flavorings to eggs and beat slightly. Pour milk mixture over egg mixture and add coconut. Pour into greased baking dish, place in pan of hot water and bake in 350 degree oven for 45 to 50 minutes. Serves 6.

P.S. I do not add the coconut when I make it for my granddaughter, because she does not like coconut. I spoil my family also. You could sprinkle coconut on top of servings for those who want it.

Gum-Drop Cookies

1/2 C. shortening
1/2 C. brown sugar
1/2 C. white sugar
1 t. vanilla
1 beaten egg
1 C. flour
1/2 t. baking powder
1/2 t. soda
1/4 t. salt
1/2 C. grated coconut or nuts
1/2 C. small gum-drops
1 C. quick cooking oatmeal

Mix the shortening, sugars and vanilla with the beaten egg. Mix the flour, soda, baking powder and salt. Stir the two mixtures together and add the coconut, gum-drops, and oatmeal. Drop by rounded teaspoon onto an oiled cookie sheet and bake 10 minutes in 350 degree oven.

Gifts from the Kitchen

They say that Grandma is not making so many cookies anymore. However, I know quite a few who are busy making their own very special cookies for gifts; candies too!

They have been saving their coffee cans to decorate and fill with goodies. It's not too early to start with our Christmas baking; all of the following gifts are good keepers, if you hide them. My children and their friends loved these:

Gifts from the Kitchen

Then I remembered this:

Gum-Drop Fruit Cake

1 C. white sugar
1 C. brown sugar
1-1/2 C. cooking oil
2 C. applesauce
2 t. soda
4 C. flour
1 C. gum-drops
1 C. dates, cut up
1 C. raisins
1 C. nuts, coarsely chopped
1 t. each of ginger, cinnamon and allspice.

Cream sugars and oil. Add applesauce, raisins, dates, gum-drops and nuts. Add flour, sifted with spices and soda. Mix well. Fill well-greased bread pans 2/3 full and bake 1-1/2 hours at 325 degrees. Makes 2 loaves.

Mamie Eisenhower's Fudge

3 C. sugar
1/2 C. margarine
2/3 C. evaporated milk

Stir and boil 5 minutes, stirring constantly. Remove from heat and add:

1 (12 oz.) package chocolate chips
1 jar (small size) of marshmallow creme
1 C. nuts
1 t. vanilla

Mix all together and pour in a 9 x 13 oiled pan. Cool and cut in desired sized pieces.

Gifts from the Kitchen

My friend, Wilma Sayles, makes fudge every year for her friends; here is her recipe for:

Gifts from the Kitchen

For peanut butter lovers, we can make this:

For those who want to cut down on sugar, these stuffed dates and prunes are delicious. I have made them for years and they are very popular.

Peanut Butter Fudge

1 C. brown sugar
1 C. white sugar
1/2 C. milk
2 T. butter
1/8 t. salt
1 C. peanut butter
4 T. light syrup
1 t. vanilla

Boil white sugar, brown sugar, milk, butter and salt to a soft boil stage (240 degrees F.) Remove from heat; add peanut butter and syrup. Stir until well mixed and add vanilla. Put into oiled pan to cool. Cut into desired sized pieces.

Stuffed Dates and Prunes

For the stuffing use equal amounts of raisins, coconut and nuts. Grind them together in the food grinder, using the finest cutter. (I have one of those little Kitchen Choppers which is good for times like this.) Two tablespoons of each will fill about 25 prunes or dates. If your prunes have pits, steam them about 5 minutes to easily remove the pits. (Most come pitted now.) Fill the dates and prunes with the nutty mixture. Roll some in powdered sugar for those with a sweet-tooth.

My Waldorf Salad

Dice apples and add lots of crisp diced celery; add a few raisins if you have them. Add chunky peanut butter to your regular salad dressing, using about half of each—you'll love it. Line your bowl with a bed of lettuce.

The Apple—Nature's Toothbrush

It is a perfect morsel at any time of the year, though they are at their zesty best now. Dentists recommend apples as a healthy snack that does not contribute to plaque formation. We even have a special dip for apples and other fruits at our markets. To make your own, do it this way:

Fruit Dip

1 pkg. (8 oz.) cream cheese, at room temperature
1 small jar marshmallow creme

Combine ingredients until creamy; we use the electric hand mixer for this. Surround it with apple slices, fresh peaches and pears, or even strawberries and cherries, and don't forget grapes. If it is too thick, carefully add a little fruit juice.

Healthful Snacks

Americans are snack people. It just overwhelms my mind when I think of the number of snacks consumed while the World Series was being played. The media gave us plenty of time to dash to the refrigerator and snack cupboard between innings. Snacks are good for us so long as we incorporate them in our dietary needs for the day. So let's save room for those healthful snacks, concentrating on luscious fruits, vegetables and cheeses. I still love a glass of milk and a cookie—an old favorite. Other old favorites include apples, peanut butter, popcorn, cheese and crackers and fresh raw vegetables and other fruits.

Did you ever spread peanut butter on crisp apple slices? Apples and peanut butter can be combined in this salad. It might not be considered a snack, but it sure has all the ingredients for one. Any time you want to make a Waldorf salad and you do not have any nuts, do it this way:

Healthful Snacks

If you want a low-calorie dip for crackers and chips, this is very tasty; nice to have on hand for a snack any time.

My daughter, Shirley, gave me this recipe years ago. She liked to have it on hand in the refrigerator for snacks or lunch box sandwiches.

Garden Dip

2/3 C. cottage cheese
1/2 T. finely grated onion
2 T. carrots, finely grated
1 T. finely chopped green pepper
1/2 t. salt
Dash of garlic powder
1 C. plain yogurt

Mash cottage cheese with a fork; add onion, carrot, green pepper, salt and garlic powder. Stir in yogurt, chill several hours. This is also good with your favorite garden vegetables.

Deviled Ham and Cheese Spread

Mix a 2-1/2 oz. can deviled ham with a 3 ounce package of cream cheese, softened, 1/2 t. lemon juice and a little horseradish to taste. That's all; spread on any kind of crackers or bread.

Baked French Toast

1 lb. loaf French bread
1/2 C. butter or margarine, softened
2/3 C. brown sugar
Cinnamon
1 C. milk
3 eggs
1/4 t. salt

Preheat oven to 350 degrees. Add milk and salt to well beaten eggs. Cut bread into 1 to 1-1/2 inch slices. Use a 10 x 15 inch jelly roll pan. Spread butter over bottom of pan and sprinkle with brown sugar and cinnamon. Let bread slices stand in egg mixture until well saturated. Place on top of butter and sugar and sprinkle with cinnamon. Bake at 350 degrees for 25 to 30 minutes. Serve with sour cream, jam or maple syrup. (From Wealtha Hedgecock of Cadillac, Michigan and Sun City, Arizona.)

Wealtha also makes this:

Fruit Salad

Put together a salad choosing from sliced oranges, grapefruit sections, thinly sliced apples, cut up peaches or nectarines, pears, and blueberries. If she wants to extend it for a crowd or wants to have some leftover for another time, she adds a can of cherry or peach pie filling. The pie filling keeps the fruit from turning dark. Salad will stay pretty and fresh in refrigerator.

Brunch

Americans are becoming a brunch generation; yet many of us can remember when we first heard the word used. Brunch is convenient; we can serve our best loved breakfast foods that we do not have the time to prepare when we are hurrying off to work. Brunch is a time for wonderful foods like omelettes, crepes, cheesy Mexican dishes, French toast or eggs benedict.

A brunch for two is fun and we know that we do not need to cook dinner later in the day. It is also great when feeding a crowd; and can be served in a casual manner when guests are ready for it. Here are some favorites from special friends.

Brunch

Kate Boice served this between Christmas and New Year's at a beautiful brunch in her home south of Indianapolis. It was accompanied by slices of ham, a fruit salad and her holiday fruit cake and cookies. This recipe has been in her family for many years.

Kate's Egg Puff

10 eggs
1/2 C. flour
1 t. salt
1 C. cottage cheese
1 lb. shredded Cheddar cheese
1/2 C. margarine or 1/4 C. margarine and 1/4 C. vegetable oil
1 t. green chilies (optional) chopped very fine
1 t. baking powder

Beat eggs until light. Add flour, baking powder, salt, cottage cheese, Cheddar cheese and melted margarine. Blend until smooth. Add chilies. Pour mixture into well-buttered 9 x 13 inch pan. Bake at 350 degrees for 35 minutes, 'til center appears firm and the top is browned. Kate says that this freezes well if you have leftovers.

Cornbread and Egg Casserole

1 (8 inch) square pan cornbread, cooled and crumbled
1-1/2 C. (6 oz.) shredded Cheddar cheese
12 slices bacon, cooked and crumbled
8 eggs
1-1/2 C. milk
1/3 C. margarine
1 T. chopped chives (if not available, use green onions)

Preheat oven to 350 degrees. Grease a 7 x 11 inch baking pan. Save 1 cup of lightly packed cornbread crumbs for the top and mix the remainder with the cheese and bacon. Lightly press into bottom of prepared dish. Make 8 evenly spaced depressions in the cornbread mixture. Break one egg in each hole. Pour milk over top of casserole. Cover loosely with foil, bake for 25 to 30 minutes or until eggs are desired doneness.

Melt margarine in skillet. Add remaining 1 cup crumbs and chives. Stir over medium heat until crumb mixture is golden grown. Sprinkle over baked casserole. Makes 6 to 8 servings according to appetites.

Brunch

This next casserole is one of my favorites; a truly American down-to-earth, stick-to-the-ribs entree. I usually make the cornbread the night before using a 7 oz. box of cornmeal muffin mix. Follow the instructions on the box.

Winter

Table of Contents

Winter

Salmon Poached in Champagne

With dill sauce

6 slices salmon about 1" thick
6 T. butter
2 T. lemon juice
1/2 C. champagne
2 T. chopped chives or green onions
Sour cream dill sauce (recipe follows)

Melt butter in a pan; add lemon juice, champagne and chives. Add salmon; baste. Cover, cook over low heat 30 minutes. Place salmon on a pretty platter and serve with this sauce:

Sour Cream Dill Sauce

1/2 C. sour cream
1 T. Dijon-style mustard
2 t. lemon juice
1 T. chopped chives
2 T. sugar
1 t. dried dill weed

Combine all ingredients in a glass jar, stir until blended. Refrigerate until serving time.

This recipe can be made with other large fish if you do not have the salmon, and dry white wine can be substituted for the champagne.

Winter

The winter solstice is almost upon us; when we have the most to do, the days become shorter and shorter. Everyone is hungry. What are we going to have for dinner?

Planning is the answer. Have your regular staples on hand and add a few things like fish, ground beef patties or cubed steaks and sausage in the freezer. I am not saying that I do this, however it does solve some problems.

To impress a special guest or two, you can even prepare and serve this exotic salmon entree with dill sauce in 45 minutes at the most. If you have forgotten to take the fish out of the freezer, you can thaw it in the microwave.

Winter

This is what you can do with those cubed steaks. One pound serves four and cubing makes it tender, even though it is low in fat. Store in the refrigerator up to 3 days or freeze in individual packages for easy thawing. Defrost in refrigerator 30 minutes or microwave on defrost 2 to 3 minutes.

Try this recipe that can be prepared in 15 minutes.

P.S. Many families would appreciate pancakes and sausage on one of these cold winter nights.

Cubo-Quicko for Two

2 beef cubed steaks
Pepper
1 T. oil
1 jar (8 ozs.) spaghetti sauce
Salt

Sprinkle both sides of steak with pepper, set aside. Heat oil in non-stick pan on medium-high heat. Cook steaks 1 to 1-1/2 minutes per side. Add salt, top with heated spaghetti sauce. Serve over your favorite pasta made according to package directions. This recipe can be doubled, easily.

Sparkling Cider Punch

Prepare the no-alcohol version with red star ice cubes for the kid's party. Offer both versions to adults.

2 quarts cranberry juice cocktail, chilled
1 quart apple cider or juice, chilled
1 bottle dry red wine, chilled (optional)
1 (1 liter) bottle ginger ale, chilled
Red star ice cubes (recipe follows) or small ice cubes

Combine cranberry juice, apple cider and red wine, if desired, in a punch bowl. Slowly add ginger ale. Carefully add ice cubes. Makes about 20 servings without wine and 26 servings with wine.

Red Star Ice Cubes

Place a cranberry in the bottom of each star shaped ice cube compartment. Add about 1/4 inch of water to each compartment. Freeze until firm. Add water to within 1/4 inch of the top. Freeze until firm. Pop out and store in the freezer in a covered container. Make as many as you wish.

Christmas

On a cold winter's night when the stars are so close that you feel you could almost touch them and the snow is crisp under your feet, there is a holiday magic in the air. It is easy to understand why the poet wrote about Santa Claus with his reindeer sailing through the sky. I hope that our computer-age children with their plastic toys will feel this mysterious magic and we will all believe in the search for "Peace on Earth."

A bright red punch is ideal for any Christmas get-together. I picked up this recipe in Wisconsin last fall where they were celebrating Warren's Cranberry Festival.

Christmas

Special breads are always welcome during the holiday season. Here are a couple made with convenience foods so very needed during these busy times. Here is a bread for any season from one of our younger generation, Linda Hausler.

I am sure that Grandma would have appreciated this breakfast bread made with crescent rolls:

Herbed Cheese Bread

1 pkg. Swiss cheese with holes (about 8 ozs.)
1 loaf French bread
1/2 lb. oleo, soft
1 t. mustard

1 t. lemon juice
2 T. grated onion
1 t. poppy seeds
1 T. Bonne Saveur (Bon apetit Seasoning)

Cut French bread not quite all the way through. Put slices of cheese between bread slices. Do not let cheese stick above top of bread. Mix oleo with remaining ingredients and spread over top of bread. Cover bread with tin foil 1/2 way up side of bread, so top is exposed. Bake at 350 degrees for 25 to 30 minutes. Serves about 8-10.

Pecan Breakfast Bread

2 (8 oz.) packages refrigerated crescent rolls
2 T. butter or margarine, melted
1/2 C. sugar
1 to 2 t. cinnamon
1/4 cup pecans (optional)
Honey Topping (recipe follows)

Unroll crescent roll dough and divide into 16 triangles. Brush with melted butter and sprinkle with a mixture of the sugar, cinnamon and pecans, if used. Roll each triangle, starting from the shorter side opposite a point and rolling toward the point. In a greased 9 x 5 x 3 inch loaf pan, place 8 of the rolls, point side down. Place remaining rolls on top of the first layer.

Bake in 350 degree oven for about 55 minutes or 'til done. Remove bread from pan; turn right side up. Prepare Honey Topping. Drizzle over warm bread. Serve warm. 8 servings.

Honey Topping

In small saucepan, combine:

1/4 C. sifted powdered sugar

2 T. honey

2 T. butter or margarine

1 t. vanilla

Heat and stir until mixture is smooth and bubbly. Stir in 1/2 C. pecan halves. Cool slightly about 15 minutes before drizzling over bread.

Pork Roast

With mustard and jelly glaze

3 to 4 lbs. boneless pork loin roast

1 C. currant or apple jelly

1/2 C. prepared mustard

Heat oven to 325 degrees. Place roast in shallow roasting pan. Stir together the jelly (heated) and mustard. Brush over pork.

Roast at 325 degrees for 45 minutes, brush again with glaze and continue to roast and glaze until 155 to 160 degrees. Let stand 10 minutes before slicing. In the meantime, add enough water to the pan to make one cup of liquid, add any remaining glaze.

In small bowl, stir together 1 tablespoon cornstarch with 1 tablespoon water; add to pan, cook and stir until clear and thickened. Season to taste. Serve with the sliced pork.

Christmas

We cannot dwell on the past, though we do need to have a congenial mixture of the old and new in our food and decorations. Down memory lane I can see our stockings hanging in front of the glowing hard coal burner. When we were old enough to give gifts as well as to receive, we had a Christmas tree. An orange was always in our stocking. A real treat. All kinds of fruits make beautiful decorations for the holidays.

I have decided to prepare a pork roast this Christmas. We have ignored pork long enough. Today's leaner pork has less fat (45% less) than 10 years ago and it is so easy to prepare.

Diets

I still like to think of New Year's Day as the morning of my year. The past is over and it is time to start a-fresh. Many of us are almost afraid to get on our scales after eating all of those goodies. So, now let's plan some reduced calorie meals that are still nutritious. We could start by serving Rock Cornish Game Hens with a beautiful raspberry sauce for New Year's dinner. One half of a small game hen is only 215 calories without the skin and is low in cholesterol and fat.

Cornish Game Hens with Raspberry Sauce

From the American Cancer Society Newsletter

3 Cornish hens
1 (10 oz. pkg.) frozen red raspberries in lite syrup, thawed
1 t. vanilla extract
1 t. cornstarch
1/4 C. water

Preheat oven to 350 degrees. Wash and drain Cornish hens. Cut hens in half. Place halves in a roasting pan, breast-side up. Roast 1 hour or until done.

Raspberry Sauce: Before the hens are finished, place raspberries in blender and blend until smooth. (Optional: push puree through sieve to remove seeds, if desired). In a pan combine the raspberry puree and vanilla. In a small jar shake the cornstarch and water. Cook the raspberry mixture and when it is hot (but not boiling) slowly add the cornstarch. Stir until slightly thickened and hot (about 8 minutes). Cover and keep warm until ready to serve. Serve on top of Cornish hens. Serves 6.

Baked Sweet Potatoes

About 2 lb. sweet potatoes or yams
1/2 C. brown sugar
butter or margarine
1/2 C. dried fine bread crumbs

Boil the potatoes in salted water until tender (if they are real large, cut them in large chunks). When cool enough to handle, peel and slice them. Put them in a shallow baking dish, sprinkle with brown sugar, crumbs. Then dot generously with butter. Bake at 350 degrees until thoroughly heated.

Diets

I am ready to make baked sweet potatoes again after having them for Thanksgiving. This recipe has fewer calories than if I had used the canned variety in heavy syrup.

Far be it from me to tell anyone to diet. However, here are some ideas if you want to be careful at the New Year's celebration:

1. *Eat a low-fat breakfast and nutritious lunch before going to a big holiday dinner. It will help you to enjoy the meal without over-indulging.*
2. *Reach for the fruit and vegetable trays and go easy on the dips.*
3. *Make your first drink mineral water or seltzer.*
4. *Sample desserts as if they were rare wines.*
5. *Take a walk instead of seconds.*

Diets

Serve with a fresh green salad using your favorite low calorie dressing, and finish your dinner with this:

Amazing Fruit Delight

From the American Cancer Society Newsletter
2 C. whole wheat bread, cut into bite-size cubes
1/3 C. toasted wheat germ
1 t. cinnamon
21 oz. can apple pie filling
1 medium banana
1 C. dried fruit (pears, prunes, apples, or apricots) chopped into small pieces
10 maraschino cherries (optional)
1/2 C. apple juice
1/3 C. honey
1/4 C. maple syrup
1 t. margarine
1 t. brown sugar

Preheat oven to 350 degrees. Put bread cubes, wheat germ, and cinnamon into a small bowl and toss gently. In a second bowl mix the pie filling, dried fruit, and mashed banana. In a fancy 9-inch pie pan place half the bread mixture. Add the fruit mixture and top with the rest of the bread mixture. Decorate the top with cherries.

In a small saucepan or microwave, heat the apple juice, honey, maple syrup, margarine, and brown sugar until warm. Pour the mixture over the fruit delight. Cover with aluminum foil and bake 30 minutes. May be served hot or cold. Serves 8.

Roast Beef

Sometimes I brown the roast in a little oil in a non-stick fry pan. Then put it in the roaster with about 1/2 cup of water. Add some chopped onions and, when I think of it, I put small slivers of garlic in a few slits made in the roast. Sprinkle with salt and pepper and roast covered for 1-1/2 to 2 hours at 325 degrees. Check for doneness and at this point I sometimes add some vegetables like carrots, onions and potatoes. Cover and bake until tender. Many times I do not add the vegetables, though we must make gravy.

Gravy

Drain off any extra fat in the roaster and add about a cup of hot water in which a bouillon cube has been dissolved. Thicken with 1 tablespoon of flour or cornstarch for every cup of liquid. Mix the flour with enough cold water to make a smooth paste, add a little of the gravy to it, then gradually add to the pot and stir constantly until smooth and of the desired thickness. Add seasoning to taste.

Beef

After all of those rich holiday meals with elegant desserts as well as candies and snacks, we are ready now for plain every day foods again. We are hungry for bread, meat and potatoes. This is where beef comes into the picture. Beef roast was often served during the depression years. Beef was cheaper than chicken in those days. Now, I hunger for one of those Sunday dinners of:

Beef Roast
Mashed Potatoes and Gravy
Coleslaw
Baked beans
Fruit Jello with whipped cream

Through the years I have acquired special utensils like electric fry pans, pressure cookers and microwaves. However, for a good beef roast, I still prefer a small enamel roaster. This little roaster has attended more pot-lucks and family picnics through the years than I wish to count.

Beef

Here is a recipe for meatball soup; a robust and tasty soup using ground beef.

Meatball Soup

Meatballs:

1-1/2 lbs. ground beef
1 egg
3 T. water
1/2 C. dry bread crumbs
1/4 t. salt
1 T. chopped parsley
2 T. butter

Combine beef, egg, water, bread crumbs, salt and parsley. Mix lightly, shape into 24 balls. In a 5 qt. Dutch oven melt butter and brown meatballs on all sides, one layer at a time. Drain off fat; remove meatballs and set aside.

Soup:

2 C. water
1 can (10-1/2 oz.) condensed beef broth, undiluted
1 envelope dry onion soup mix (1-3/4 oz.)
1 C. sliced carrots
1/4 C. chopped celery tops
1/4 C. chopped parsley
1 t. pepper
1/4 t. dried oregano
1/4 t. dry basil
1 bay leaf

Combine all the ingredients in the same Dutch oven. Bring to boil. Reduce heat and simmer for 20 minutes. Add meatballs and simmer 20 minutes longer. Makes about 2 quarts.

Tortilla Burgers

Spread hot tortillas with hot refried beans. Top with shredded lettuce, cooked beef patty, pour over this a mild taco sauce; top with a fried egg and shredded Cheddar cheese.

Beef

Friends from the ski slopes will be hungry enough for these:

Super Bowl

Super Bowl is one "Holiday" of the year when there is no time to sit down to a family dinner; yet food is very much in demand. A meal cannot be set for a specific time; we are never sure just when half-time will begin. Start with a big breakfast before the kick-off. Most game watchers that I know are very good at fixing their own favorites, like omelets and Eggs Benedict. Then make a big dish of soup to have handy in the slow cooker. This soup will serve 8 to 10 TV watchers.

A Glorified Potato Soup

About 2 lbs. or 6 medium potatoes, peeled and cubed
1 medium onion, chopped
1/2 C. chopped celery
1/2 C. chopped carrot
2 T. butter or margarine
2 T. cornstarch
8 C. milk
2 T. instant chicken bouillon granules
4 C. shredded American cheese (16 ozs.)
1-1/2 C. chopped fully cooked ham (8 oz.)

Cook potatoes in a saucepan with enough water to cover until just tender. Drain off water. In soup kettle or Dutch oven, cook onion, celery and carrot in butter until tender. Stir in cornstarch. Add the milk and bouillon granules to the cooked onion mixture. Stir in potatoes and cook until slightly thickened. Stir in the cheese and ham until cheese is melted. If you wish, put in the slow cooker set on low until needed.

Pizza Cups

3/4 lb. ground beef
1 can (6 ozs.) tomato paste
1 T. instant minced onion
1 t. Italian seasoning
1/2 t. salt
1 can (10 ozs.) refrigerated biscuits
1/2 to 1/3 cups shredded mozzarella cheese

Brown and drain beef. Stir in tomato paste, onion and seasonings (mixture will be thick). Cook over low heat for five minutes, stirring frequently. Place biscuits in a greased muffin tin, pressing to cover bottom and sides. Spoon about 1/4 cup of meat mixture into biscuit lined cups and sprinkle with cheese. Bake at 400 degrees for 12 minutes or until golden brown. Makes 12 pizza cups.

Super Bowl

We can send out for our favorite pizzas or make these special Pizza Cups. They are a quickie and can be baked in 12 minutes.

Super Bowl

Super Bowl is a big day for munchies, and our favorite family dips. A number of years ago Tony Hedgecock gave me the following recipe. He said that he made this dip in Garmish, Germany and ski training camps throughout the United States as a coach for U.S. Olympic teams.

My granddaughter, Carla, makes this dip and it does not take long for it all to disappear at our family gatherings. So easy and so good!

Tony's Guacamole Dip

3 medium sized avocados, ripe and soft
1 large fresh tomato, finely diced
1 very small sweet onion, diced
Salsa sauce to taste
Garlic powder or fresh garlic (1 t. powder or 1 clove of garlic, squeezed)
1 t. chili powder
Juice of 1/4 fresh lime
Dash of salt

Mash avocado well, add the finely diced tomato and onion and seasonings. Squeeze lime juice over all and mix well. Taste and add a little salt if needed.

Tony says to be sure to use unflavored tortilla chips with this dip as cheese or other flavored chips will detract from the delicious flavor of this sauce.

Carla's Cheese Dip

1 pkg. (8 ozs.) Mexica Velveeta, Mild
1 (15 ozs.) can Hormel Chili No Beans

Cube the cheese and mix with the chili in a microwave safe bowl. Microwave on high stirring often until hot. Serve hot with chips, all kinds of crisp veggies and toasted French bread slices.

This fun day can be a happy time regardless of who wins. In fact, I think that we are all winners on Super Bowl Day!

Marinara Sauce

Makes 1-1/2 cups
1 minced garlic clove
2 tablespoons olive oil and oil from anchovies
2-1/2 cups squished Italian tomatoes
6 finely chopped anchovies
1/2 teaspoon oregano
1 tablespoon chopped parsley
Parmesan cheese

Saute garlic lightly in olive oil and anchovy oil. Stir in tomatoes, anchovies, oregano and parsley. Simmer 15 to 20 minutes uncovered. Serve on cooked pasta and top with Parmesan cheese.

Pasta

From Don Taylor's menu for his about-to-open Italian restaurant:

"Pasta has always been the glory of Italian food, and a symbol of Italian national pride. Today, Italian pasta delights the world . . . In Italy, pasta is served as an entree before the meat course, while outside of Italy it is frequently thought of as a main course itself, and served with simply a salad. Italian cooks criticize foreign cooks for 'ruining' authentic Italian dishes by drowning the pasta in sauce. The sauce is literally a sauce, intended to coat the pasta and add its flavor to every mouthful."

Italians fuss over perfectly cooked pasta as the French over a souffle or the English over well-made tea. Pasta should always be firm and provide some resistance or bite.

Here is Don's recipe for Marinara Sauce.

Pasta

Here is a pasta dish that could become a family favorite.

Quick Cheddar Bake

8 oz. small shell pasta
2 T. each butter and flour
1-1/4 C. milk
2-1/2 C. grated Cheddar cheese, divided
2 oz. ham, cut in thin strips or chunks
1/2 C. chopped scallions
Salt and freshly ground pepper to taste

Cook pasta according to package directions, drain and set aside. Heat oven to 350 degrees. In small saucepan melt butter over medium heat, add flour. Cook, stirring 2 minutes. Add milk and cook stirring until thickened. Add 1 cup cheese. Combine this sauce with shells, 1 cup cheese, ham, scallions and seasonings. Place in large casserole or a few smaller ones. Top with remaining cheese. Bake until browned and bubbly, about 10 minutes.

Joey's Extra Cheesy Pasta

1 (7 oz.) pkg. macaroni and cheese dinner
1 (16 oz.) can tomatoes, cut up
1 (8 oz.) pkg. thin sliced corned beef
1 (8 oz.) pkg. sliced Swiss cheese

Make the macaroni and cheese according to directions on the box. Add the chopped tomatoes. Put the mixture in a shallow baking dish, cover with the slices of corned beef, then the Swiss cheese slices. Bake in a 375 degree oven until bubbly and cheese melts. Serve with warm bread and a salad.

It is easy to understand the Italians for their national pride in good food. This is what the early immigrants loved to hear from Angelo M. Pellegrini:

"We are children of the oldest civilization in the Western world. We came to America to earn our bread with pick and shovel. But we can hold our heads high. . . We are the breed of Dante, da Vinci and Michelangelo."

Pasta

Next is one of my put-togethers which includes the favorite ingredients enjoyed by my grandson.

Valentine's Day

Valentine's Day is a good time to invite a few friends in for a luncheon or afternoon tea. We need something a little special these winter days. It is easy to become a mite dormant when the snow continues to fall and the sun shines only a few hours a day if we are lucky.

When Mother wanted something delicate and fancy, she made tarts; they were irresistible. She made them from her regular pie crust dough and filled them with fruit preserves, jellies and jams. This pie crust will make 12 tart shells.

Baked Tart Shells

1-1/2 C. flour
1 T. sugar
1/4 t. salt
1/3 C. shortening
3-4 T. cold water

Mix flour, sugar and salt in medium bowl with fork. Cut in shortening with pastry blender or two knives. Sprinkle in cold water, 1 tablespoon at a time, until pastry holds together. Shape into ball; divide into 12 equal pieces. Carefully shape into a ball; roll into circles about 5 inches in diameter. Press into tart pans or muffin pans that are 3 x 1-1/2 inches deep; prick bottom with a fork. Bake in 425 degree oven 10 to 12 minutes or until light golden brown. If using a recipe for unbaked shells, do not prick the bottom.

For baked shells, fill them with jams, jellies or chilled sauces and custards.

Lemon Tarts

1-1/3 C. sweetened condensed milk
1/2 C. lemon juice
2 egg yolks

Blend until thickened, fill cooled tart shells

Baby Tart Shells

1 C. flour
1 pkg. (3 ozs.) cream cheese
1/2 C. butter

Beat butter and cream cheese until smooth; work in flour until well blended. Press small amount of dough into sides of small tart tins; prick with fork. Bake in 325 degree oven 20 to 25 minutes.

Pecan Filling

1 egg
1 C. brown sugar
1 t. vanilla
Broken pecans

Beat egg, brown sugar and vanilla until smooth. Drop a few broken pecans in bottom of unbaked tart shell. Top with a teaspoon of filling. Do not prick if using unbaked shells. Bake in 325 degree oven 20 to 25 minutes. Watch to see that they do not brown too quickly.

Valentine's Day

Here is a delicious and easy filling to make for baked shells:

These pecan tarts are very easy to make. I use the baby size muffin tins for these shells.

Valentine's Day

If you are serving luncheon, I would like to recommend Irene Hennessey's:

Tator-Tot Casserole

Layer 2 lbs. ground beef in 9 x 13 inch casserole or pan; season with salt and pepper. Add layer of chopped onion, a large bag of frozen vegetables, 2 cans cream of chicken soup, a layer of sliced American cheese and cover with a layer of Tator-Tots. Bake 350 degrees for 1-1/2 hours or in 325 degree oven if using a glass pan. Makes 8 to 10 servings.

This can be made early in the day and baked just before serving. Irene browns the meat before putting it in the pan. This removes the grease.

Serve a colorful tray of relishes with this casserole, and add a variety of tarts for dessert; a delightful Valentine luncheon to remember.

Martha Washington's Fruit Cake

1 lb. butter
2-1/2 C. sugar
3 eggs
4 C. flour
3 lbs. currants
2 lbs. raisins
1-1/4 lbs. citron
1 lb. hickory nuts
1 C. water
1/4 C. brandy
1 T. cloves
2 T. powdered cinnamon
3 t. mace
3 t. nutmeg

Blend butter and sugar. Add beaten eggs and flour; set aside. Make another mixture of fruits and nuts. Add water mixed with brandy. Sprinkle spices over the mixture; combine thoroughly with the first mixture. Bake in well-greased loaf pans in 325 degree oven 2 hours.

Patriotism

February inspires us to take time to honor our patriots. What is patriotism? Perhaps it can be best described with George Washington's simple virtues of honesty and courage, a tremendous force of character with great dignity and a sense of moderation—the picture of a great patriotic man. Personally, I still get misty-eyed when our flag passes by and I like to think that it is universal.

I am sure that Martha Washington was not able to spend too much time in the kitchen. When she married George Washington she owned 7,000 acres of cultivated land, the same amount of woodland, as well as $100,000 in gold. However, her recipes were in the early cookbooks and she was famous for her hospitality and her food.

Patriotism

We must have one cherry recipe to honor George and his cherry tree. Our forefathers must have had a "sweet tooth," as desserts were an important part of the daily meals, and puddings were very popular. This is an old recipe that I have up-dated with modern measurements and methods.

Cherry Pudding

1 can pitted dark sweet cherries or home canned
1/4 C. butter
1 C. biscuit mix
1/4 t. nutmeg
2 T. sugar
1/3 C. milk

Drain the cherries reserving the juice for the sauce. Melt the butter in a 2 quart baking dish. Mix the biscuit mix, sugar and nutmeg; add the milk stirring good with a fork. Put this mixture into the baking dish over the butter. Spoon the cherries over the center. Bake in a 350 degree oven about 35 minutes or until a knife inserted in the center comes out clean.

Meanwhile make this:

Cherry Sauce

Add enough water to the drained juice to make 1-1/2 cups. Bring to a boil, then add:
2 T. cornstarch, dissolved in 1/2 C. cold water
Add 3 tablespoons sugar, 1/8 t. salt, 2 t. lemon juice and 1 tablespoon butter. Cook until thick, stirring constantly.

Let the pudding set 10 minutes before serving. Pour the sauce over it. A dab of whipped topping is nice, though not necessary.

Baked Indian Pudding

1/3 C. cornmeal
1/2 C. molasses
Pinch of salt
3 C. scalded milk
1 egg, beaten
1 C. raisins
1/4 t. ginger
1/4 t. cinnamon
1/4 t. nutmeg
1 C. cold milk

Mix cornmeal, molasses and salt well. Pour scalded milk over the mixture; let stand 5 minutes. Add well-beaten egg, spices and raisins. Put in baking dish; place in 275 degree oven. Add 1 cup of cold milk 10 minutes after it starts to bake, stir, bake 2 hours.

Patriotism

Then there is "Honest Abe." The public does not give a name like that to just anyone. It was the patriot, Abraham Lincoln, who kept our nation united.

We can be sure that his favorite foods would be plain midwest fare like side pork, sauerkraut, bean soup, fried potatoes or cornbread, and pie, of course. Foods from his Indiana and Illinois upbringing. I imagine that he often ate this pudding:

Quick One-Dish Meals

"As the days begin to lengthen, the cold begins to strengthen" and it is soup time in our North Country. Now is the time to prepare good nourishing quick meals when the family comes in out of the cold. They will relish this chowder and one can prepare it in a little over one-half hour. It's a complete meal; serve it with crackers and fruit for dessert. Our ancestors from New England would probably have an apple pie on hand. I made it with frozen Chinook salmon using just one half of the ingredients for about 2 quarts of the delicious chowder.

There is nothing better than a fluffy hot baked potato on a cold day. If you are in a hurry, bake them in the microwave. They become a complete meal when surrounded with these toppings:

Great Lakes Fish Chowder

1/2 C. butter or margarine, divided
3 medium onions, sliced
5 medium potatoes, peeled and diced
4 t. salt
1/2 t. pepper
3 C. boiling water

2 pounds fresh or frozen King salmon or frozen haddock fillets, cut into large chunks
1 qt. milk, scalded
1 can (12 oz.) evaporated milk

In a 6 to 8 quart kettle, melt 1/4 cup butter over medium heat. Saute onions until tender but now browned. Add potatoes, salt, pepper and water. Top with fish. Simmer, covered, 25 minutes or until potatoes are fork-tender. Stir in scalded milk, evaporated milk and remaining butter; heat through. Season with additional salt and pepper if desired.

Baked Potato Toppings   (2 servings)

Chef's Sauce

1/4 C. sour cream
2 T. soft margarine or butter
1/2 C. shredded sharp Cheddar cheese
1 T. chopped chives (optional)

Combine sour cream, margarine, cheese and chives in small bowl. Spoon over hot baked potatoes.

Mock Sour Cream

(2 servings)

1 C. cottage cheese, pureed
1 t. prepared horseradish
Minced parsley

Other Toppings

Peanuts, whole or chopped
Chopped dried beef
Chopped cooked bacon
Chopped onion
Sunflower seeds
Grated Cheeses

Amish Meal-In-One

2 lb. hamburger
Salt and pepper to taste
A little brown sugar
1/4 onion, chopped
1 can tomato soup, undiluted

1 can cream of chicken soup, undiluted
1 pkg. (16 oz.) egg noodles
1 pkg. (8 oz.) processed cheese

Brown hamburger with salt, pepper, brown sugar and onion. Add tomato soup. Cook egg noodles, drain. Add cream of chicken soup to noodles. Layer hamburger mixture and noodle mixture in casserole dish with processed cheese between layers.

Bake at 350 degrees for 1/2 hour.

Quick One-Dish Meals

I really like this recipe for a quick one-dish meal from our Amish friends. . .

Quick One-Dish Meals

For dessert for any of these easy, nutritious meals, I would like to suggest this delicious fruity combination. . .

Ambrosia

(Serves 4 to 6)

1 can (20 oz.) pineapple chunks in juice
1 can (11 oz.) mandarin orange segments
1 banana, peeled and sliced
1-1/2 cups seedless grapes
1 cup miniature marshmallows
1/2 cup flaked coconut
1/4 cup chopped almonds
1 carton (8 oz.) vanilla yogurt

Drain pineapple and oranges and retain juice to use as a beverage. Combine oranges, pineapple, banana, grapes, marshmallows, coconut and almonds.

Fold in yogurt and chill.

Snickers

12 ozs. low-fat vanilla ice cream or vanilla frozen yogurt
1 C. cool whip
1 pkg. (3 ozs.) instant chocolate pudding
1/4 C. crunchy peanut butter
1/3 to 1/2 C. Grapenuts

Mix all ingredients except the Grape Nuts together in large bowl until thoroughly mixed; add Grape Nuts.

Put in 8 x 8 inch glass dish; freeze one hour. Cut into bars; wrap each bar. Freeze. 8 servings.

From Marianne Halstad, Zearing, Iowa. Marianne puts hers in 8 clear plastic cups with covers to freeze.

Kid's Cooking

I am happy to see that the new homes center around the kitchen and youngsters are fixing their own snacks. They enjoy using the beautiful modern equipment; like me, they are fascinated with all of them.

Kid's love to make sandwiches and it is amazing to discover the ingenuity in the making of a sandwich by our modern kids from tots to teens. I think that cooking gives boys and girls confidence in other things they do and they are inspired.

They will enjoy making the following snickers. It will be a good lesson in measuring ingredients, and no special equipment is required nor is there any cooking on the stove. Grown-ups love them also and they are low in cholesterol and fat; yet so good.

Kid's Cooking

All young children in my acquaintance love grilled cheese sandwiches and tomato soup. It does not take long to learn how to use the electric can opener for the soup or to make:

Every young cook needs the thrill of removing something beautiful from the oven. Why not start with:

Grilled Cheese Sandwiches

Put one or two slices of cheese between two slices of bread. Butter the outside of the sandwich (it's not needed inside). Grill over medium heat on a non-stick griddle or skillet until golden brown. Always serve these sandwiches with your favorite kind of pickle.

Cornmeal Muffins

Make them from a mix, following the directions on the package. They are a favorite of all ages and so good with tomato soup. Serve with lots of butter and strawberry jam.

I believe that any good food deserves a pretty setting. The table should be worthy of the food served, so decorate it a little for the young cooks. Make it a fun meal; they will be inspired.

Fish Boil

Cut large fish (salmon or trout) in steak size pieces. Using a very large kettle (a 10 qt. or canner will do) fill half full with water. Bring to a boil. Add potatoes, after they come to a boil, cook for 12 minutes. Add small whole onions and cook for 6 minutes. Add fish steaks and 3/4 cup salt, cook for 11 minutes. Some of this salt can be put in when you start the potatoes. Total time: 29 minutes of boiling, everything comes out at the same time.

From Diane Still, Petoskey, Michigan.

Seafoods

Before there were frozen food sections in our grocery stores, we bought fresh fish packed in ice, salted codfish in little wooden boxes and oysters during the "R" months. Canned salmon, tuna fish and shrimp were good buys. We made salmon loaf, patties and salads; we breaded canned shrimp and fried them. Oyster stew was a specialty during the holidays.

We still have "Fish Boil" in our Great Lakes area. It has almost become a tradition. I make it sometimes for myself and a couple of friends using our Lake Michigan Chinook Salmon. It helps to have friends who like to fish.

This recipe sounds incredible, however, those lucky ones who sample it recommend it, and the fish comes out firm and does not absorb the salt. Keep the water boiling. Use your own amounts of ingredients depending upon the number of people you cook for and how hungry they will be.

Seafoods

If you have any fish leftover, it makes a delicious salad with lots of crisp celery, chopped onions, a little chopped sweet pickles and salad dressing.

Now our children know a lot more about our gifts from the sea, they have acquired tastes for all kinds of sea foods. They love shrimp. Try this:

Or this simple casserole dish:

Shrimp Stir-fry

Add pineapple chunks, fresh or canned, to prepared cooked shrimp. Flavor with your favorite stir-fry sauce or a bit of soy and Worcestershire sauce. Stir until heated through and serve over rice.

Shrimp and Corn Pie

2 C. corn, grated from cob or 1 can of corn, drained
2 eggs, slightly beaten
1 T. butter
1/2 C. milk
1 C. cooked shrimp
1 t. Worcestershire sauce
Salt and pepper to taste

To corn, add eggs, butter, milk, shrimp and seasoning. Bake in buttered casserole in 300 degree oven for 30 minutes. Serves 6.

Pecan Butter Rolls

From "Cooking by Touch." Makes 2 dozen.

1 C. butter or margarine
1/2 C. powdered sugar
1 t. vanilla
2 C. flour
1 C. chopped pecans
Powdered sugar

Preheat oven to 400 degrees. Cream together butter, sugar and vanilla. Mix in flour and nuts. Blend thoroughly. Form dough into 1-inch balls. Place on a lightly greased cookie sheet 2 inches apart. Bake in 400 degree oven for 20 minutes. Roll in powdered sugar while still warm.

Then another make-ahead recipe from "Cooking by Touch":

Best Nut Bread

3 C. sifted flour
1 C. sugar
4 t. baking powder
1-1/2 t. salt
1 egg, beaten
1-1/2 C. milk
2 T. salad oil
3/4 C. chopped walnuts

Preheat oven to 350 degrees. Sift first 4 ingredients together. Combine egg, milk and salad oil. Add to dry ingredients, beating well. Stir in nuts. Pour into greased 5 x 9 x 3-inch loaf pan. Bake in a 350 degree oven for 1 hour.

Coffee

It's ten o'clock in the morning and I am enjoying my second cup of coffee while watching the birds that are coming to my feeder. I count this time of day as one of my many blessings, a time to think of times past and present while deciding what I will do today.

Coffee time is a friendly time; when we meet a friend on the street any time of day is time for a cup of coffee.

Coffee time is for pleasure and relaxing; a time to take a break alone or to invite a neighbor or other friends with whom we have been out of touch.

This next recipe for pecan rolls is easy to make and to have on hand when the urge for a coffee break comes upon us. If you have these rolls in your freezer, zap them just a few seconds in the microwave.

Coffee

Then there are some delicious desserts made with coffee like this:

Coffee-Raisin Rice Pudding

1 C. packaged pre-cooked rice
1 C. coffee
1/2 C. golden raisins
1/2 C. chopped walnuts
Dash of salt
1/8 t. nutmeg
1/2 C. packed light-brown sugar
1 C. heavy cream, whipped or two cups whipped topping

Prepare rice according to package directions using coffee instead of water. Stir in remaining ingredients, except the last one, and mix well. Chill. Fold in whipped cream, reserving enough for decoration. Put in large bowl or individual serving dishes and top with remaining cream.

Brandied Coffee Jelly

2 Envelopes unflavored gelatin
2 C. hot strong coffee
1/2 C. sugar
2 T. lemon juice
2 T. brandy
Sour Cream Sauce (recipe follows)

Soften gelatin in 1/2 cup cold water. Add hot coffee and sugar and stir until sugar and gelatin are dissolved. Add lemon juice and brandy, pour into 8" square pan and chill several hours or until firm. Cut into cubes and serve with the sauce. Makes 4 to 6 servings.

Sour Cream Sauce:

Combine 1 cup dairy sour cream, 1/4 cup packed light brown sugar and 1/8 t. cinnamon. Beat until sugar is dissolved.

Coffee

Your guests and family will love this:

Alphabetical Listing of Recipes

Fall

Alphabetical Listing of Recipes

Alphabetical Listing of Recipes